AMAZON AUTOPILOT

Amazon Autopilot: How to Start an Online Business with Fulfillment by Amazon (FBA), and Let Them Do the Work

First published in 2013 by Mastery Media.
Second edition published December 2014.
Third edition published November 2015.

ISBN 978-0-984-28448-1

www.FBAmastery.com

fbamastery@gmail.com

Contents

	Date	Ordered Product Sales	Units Ordered
☐	08/01/2012	$14,245.17	702
☐	09/01/2012	$10,262.41	532
☐	10/01/2012	$12,685.62	1,062
☐	11/01/2012	$14,896.66	1,260
☐	12/01/2012	$19,117.19	1,224
	Total	$138,150.62	8,985

The numbers don't lie: Over $130,000 in sales my first year with FBA.

Introduction

I started selling on Amazon in 2007. I remember buying books based solely on intuition, and being right often enough to come out ahead most of the time. At that time the online used book market wasn't yet crowded enough to drive the price down on everything, and it wasn't unlikely you could etch out a small amount of profit from the average book.

I began to watch the guys with PDA scanners get most of the gems, as an influx of new sellers began to crowd Amazon. In short time, I bought my own scanning equipment to compete. The technology changed everything: Scan barcodes, get the rank and price info instantly, and make a buying decision. It was vastly more efficient than the old way, and my inventory and sales slowly climbed over the next three years.

By the time I moved to my current town, I had hit a ceiling. I was spending several hours a night packing orders and another hour at the post office, on top of my daily inventory shopping regimen. It was dangerously close to a "full time job" — exactly what I'd started selling on Amazon to avoid.

Then I discovered FBA. The next year, my sales more than doubled.

Fulfillment by Amazon (FBA) is little understood, and even less publicized. I wrote this book both as an instruction manual for launching your FBA empire, and to correct misconceptions among existing sellers. Among the myths:

- It is impossible to make good money selling books and media with FBA.
- The pricing benefits of FBA are limited to pricing $3.99 higher than non-FBA sellers.
- Selling with FBA means accepting the benefits at the expense of profits.

As I write this intro, I'm about to leave on a two-month road trip funded entirely by FBA. My business will be run with a laptop, smart phone, and barcode scanner. I will locate proven sources along the way, and assemble my shipments in hotel rooms and friends' living rooms. In a few days, I will set out to create a lifetime of memories that would be impossible without portability and freedom of an FBA-based business.

Let Amazon Autopilot be your blueprint for an FBA empire, and a new level of freedom.

Peter Valley

THE BLUEPRINT: BUILDING YOUR FBA EMPIRE

1

FBA EXPLAINED
FBA ADVANTAGES: TOP 10 LIST
MY FBA JOURNEY
UNDERSTANDING THE AMAZON PRIME CUSTOMER

THE BLUEPRINT: ROAD MAP TO AN FBA EMPIRE

We're going to build you an FBA empire.

First, we're going to get you the equipment to see profit everywhere.

Then we're going to automate the better part of your business, outsourcing all shipping and customer service to Amazon while increasing your profit per item.

Then we're going to teach you a systematic approach to building inventory with very little start-up capital.

Then we're going to set you loose on scorched earth missions across your town vacuuming up profitable inventory and feeding a steady stream into Amazon's warehouses.

You'll be making money in your sleep by the time you finish this book.

THE ELEGANT MONEY MACHINE

In more detail, this is the elegant money machine we will be building for you in these steps:

1. *Acquiring the hardware.* You will be purchasing, borrowing, or hustling an Android device or iPhone. You will purchase a Scanfob micro-barcode scanner. You will get your hands on a Dymo label printer.
2. *Building the infrastructure.* You will sign up for an FBA account, a scouting program, and an inventory listing program.
3. *Sourcing the inventory.* You will be unleashed with a road map for locating profitable merchandise which you send steadily to Amazon's warehouses while they do the rest of the work.

We will be starting you with books and other media as a simple, high-margin gateway. Eventually everything with a barcode will be your potential victim to be fed into the FBA money machine. You will create a localized network of sources you can visit week after week, eventually removing the guesswork and creating a calibrated system that stays in perpetual motion.

You will build an inventory to a level that will allow you to take month-long

8

vacations without working as you make money from beaches to two-lane Montana highways (I've done both in the last three months). Your automated revenue system will be in motion and Amazon will flow you money whether you're feeding it new merchandise or drinking coffee on your patio.

We are at an early stage in a major e-commerce breakthrough. You can now leverage all the resources of the largest e-commerce store in the world – its loyal customers, its loss-leader shipping rates, and its traffic as the 5th biggest website in the world (and the #1 for shopping). You have done absolutely nothing to contribute to Amazon's ascendancy, but you will be reaping many of the benefits as you build your FBA empire.

THE FIVE STEPS BETWEEN YOU AND MONEY

These are the steps between you and your first Amazon payment:

- You open an Amazon seller's account and select the "FBA" option.
- You source inventory.
- You label and send new or used products to Amazon.
- Customers buy your items.
- Amazon picks your products from inventory, then packages and ships them to the customer.

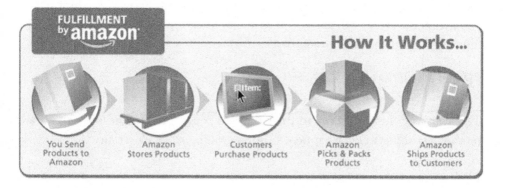

WHAT IS FBA?

In one sentence: Fulfillment by Amazon (FBA) is the ultimate automation and online sales tool.

This is how it was done the old way: You stored hundreds or thousands of

9

items in your garage or closet. You spent sometimes hours a day packing books and hauling them to the post office. It was taxing, laborious, and time consuming.

FBA is the next level: Send everything to Amazon in large shipments and let them handle it from there.

In the old way, to sell in most non-media categories, you had to prove yourself over months or years to qualify for "Featured Merchant" status, making it almost impossible to sell in most categories profitably.

With FBA, "Featured Merchant" status is built-in, expanding your potential inventory to nearly everything with a barcode. Imagine going from running a comic book store to being handed the key to your own Wal Mart.

As an FBA seller, you will be sourcing inventory—almost any inventory you want now—and shipping it to an Amazon warehouse, where they will safely store it until it sells. You will list this inventory for sale on Amazon. When it sells, your inventory will be packed and shipped by Amazon.

They will get a larger cut of the sale than if you sold it merchant-fulfilled, but you will be selling at prices higher than other sellers, and leveraging Amazon's free shipping and Prime services to attract customers willing to pay that higher price. The outsourcing of all post-transactional work (shipping + customer service) will allow you to focus solely on your new focus in life: hunting down profitable inventory.

FBA: THE TRIPLE-WIN

These are the three benefits to FBA that are key to understanding why it may be the best thing to ever happen to online selling since electricity.

FBA allows you to charge more.

On every book, you will charge **at least** $3.99 more than the lowest non-FBA seller. Even with this markup, you'll still claim the top listing on the product page. This is because listings are sorted by price plus shipping. Amazon assumes the buyer will use the free shipping option, and gives FBA sellers the top spot. Even better, you can consistently charge $5, $10, and even $20 (and more) above the lowest non-FBA price and still get sales. This is because you can offer things other sellers can't, like free second-day shipping.

FBA increases the range of profitable inventory by 99%.

Easily 80% of all media items that are profitable when sold via FBA are not profitable at merchant-fulfilled prices. FBA allows you to profitably sell not just otherwise valueless media, but anything with a bar code—from inflatable swimming pools to Clif Bars. And you instantly receive "Featured Merchant" status, elevating you to the top of the listings and out of the "below the fold" ghetto where no one is selling anything.

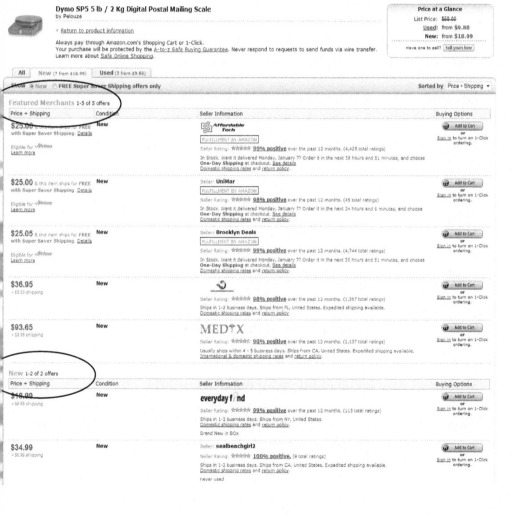

Amazon handles all shipping and customer service.

Removing this time drain from the process allows you to focus on one thing: sourcing. Authors don't bind their books; DJs don't press their vinyl. You shouldn't be stuffing envelopes. You're a sourcing machine – that's it.

DOWNSIDES OF FBA

The short answer is, there aren't any.

If you pressed people to complain, this is what you might hear:

Loss of control over order processing.
My response: Thank god.

Handing over customer service to Amazon.
My response: Take my customer service, please.

Possibility of loss or damage to your products.
My response: Rare and offset by increased sales volume.

Over-entitled, bratty customers.
My response: FBA is guilty. But worth the trouble.

More returns.
My response: More sales always means more returns.

Higher fees than listing yourself.
My response: Offset by the ability to charge more per item.

Risk of paying storage fees for items that don't sell.
My response: An extra 1 to 2 cents a month. Wow.

Massive charge for changing your mind about FBA.
My response: If you want to jump ship, you will have to pay Amazon to ship everything back to you. This can be a problem. Yet this is the kind of exotic scenario that just doesn't play out in real life often.

FBA: WHY EVERYONE DOESN'T USE IT

Three reasons:

The biggest reason for FBA-aversion among online sellers is good news in disguise: FBA is *not* easy to learn. Labeling is a project. Packing shipments is confusing. Pricing is complicated. The FBA interface is not intuitive. It's a crazy mess. But if you can weather the storm, there are fertile fields on the other side. The greater the barriers to entry, the greater the rewards that await those who clear them. If FBA was easy, everyone would do it. And you don't want that.

The second is overhead. As will be covered, it's going to cost about $280 a month to keep it afloat. This pretty much requires that your Amazon business be a level above something done in just your free time.

The third is misconceptions about fees. The hype about increased fees is true. But the conversation usually misses the point. Most Amazon sellers can't look two or three steps ahead and see the hidden benefits. I sat across the table from an experienced Amazon seller in Waffle House and told him every important thing I'm going to tell you in this book, and heard him dismiss it all with a wave and one line: "I'll never take $5 for a $10 book!"

As a triple-win for online sellers, it begs the question: Why doesn't everyone use FBA? Don't concern yourself with trying to understand. Just enjoy your bigger piece of the pie.

DAWN OF A NEW ERA: EVOLVE OR DIE

The used-goods e-commerce market is changing. We've seen what happened to eBay with a glut of merchandise turning a formerly profitable-yet-quaint online yard sale into something akin to the trading floor of the stock exchange done at a Chinese port. And I've watched it happen to Amazon.

Today, it is virtually impossible to make money with used books, music, or movies on Amazon. I feel like I caught the tail end of the glory days when I started selling (very part time) in 2007. Today, it's well past saturation point. Those who make a living off media are specializing in textbooks, selling new items bought wholesale, or sifting through used items they can pass off as new. Making a sustainable income off used media means a very undignified life of fighting for the crumbs.

Witness the rise of FBA – selling used media at a profit has arisen from the grave. Now, you've shifted your target market from the average buyer to the Amazon Prime buyer – from those willing to spend $4 for a book to someone willing to spend $12 for the same book.

With FBA, selling used media has become profitable again.

BOOKS & MEDIA: THE GATEWAY DRUG

Why books and media? Because it's easy.

We're going to give you early momentum by starting you with easily sourced merchandise that you can flip quickly with high margins: books, CDs, DVDs, and other media. Once hooked, you will expand to categories and sources with virtually no ceiling, selling not just media but anything with a barcode.

Focusing this book on media will allow us to explore the building of your FBA money machine into a concise system—and will keep this book to a manageable size.

Later, you will plug additional money-making models into the FBA framework. Among the possibilities are retail arbitrage, wholesale non-media sourcing, and importing from China.

THE AUTOMATED SALES MACHINE

Those who have read *The Four Hour Workweek*—or practiced the business architecture Timothy Ferriss lays out—will appreciate the appeal and elegance of a largely automated business. It's one that leverages someone else's technologies and platforms to sell your products. This type of business, making you money in your sleep or from a laptop anywhere in the world, has only very recently been an option.

Millions have read Ferriss's book, but one of the greatest advancements in automated businesses emerged since its publication. It is one of the most magical partially-passive income devices in the toolbox of those chasing the laptop lifestyle. Fulfillment by Amazon (FBA) puts your Internet business on a form of autopilot steroids.

The first wave of autopilot Internet models often emphasized the use of "drop shippers," which took one through a shady and muddled landscape of order fulfillment options that didn't leave much room for profit.

This is the second wave. And FBA is at the core.

THE RELUCTANT OUTSOURCER:
HOW I LEARNED TO LOVE NEVER GOING TO THE POST OFFICE

I'm kind of a lone wolf in the Amazon game, but I have a few friends who sell on Amazon. The first time I mentioned FBA to each one of them, the conversation always went the same:

"FBA? I looked into it…" followed by one or more of the following: "The fees are too much." Or, "I'm fine going to the post office." Or, "It seems like a scam."

At first inquiry, I was just as guilty. "The fees are really high" was exactly the FBA narrative I bought into. I wouldn't be corrected for many months, costing me many hundreds of unnecessary hours of labor and lost revenue in the meantime. I continued to spend hours packing books every night on the floor of my condo, losing my scissors after every book, getting tape stuck to my sweatshirt, and cutting more than a few holes in the carpet when it got so late I didn't know where the packing slip ended and the rug began.

At some point my girlfriend and I had a two-month long road trip planned, taking us through the forgotten and disrespected parts of the country: North Dakota, Montana, Wyoming, and six other states. I would often put my business on "vacation" mode for my frequent trips, but two months was too long to not have money coming in. I sat down and decided to run the numbers on switching the whole business to FBA.

My first (and only) stop was Amazon's "FBA Revenue Calculator". You enter an item and a theoretical selling price, and it shows you exactly what you would make selling it via FBA versus merchant fulfilled.

The numbers will make anyone cringe and say "no way" (refer to the chapter on FBA fees for more detail on why). As a quick refresher, a copy of *The Four Hour Workweek* sold for $9.99 will net you $8.69 when sold merchant fulfilled. When sold via FBA, you'll pocket $5.76.

That sale via FBA comes at a loss of 44% compared to the merchant-fulfilled sale. Multiply by 500 books a month, and you're dealing with numbers most people would be thrilled to stand in post office lines every day to avoid.

The "FBA Revenue Calculator" is most people's first stop when considering FBA. Ostensibly, this is a tool to sell Amazon sellers on signing up. In reality, I think this tool has done more to dissuade people from trying FBA than any other single influence. Because it doesn't reveal the hidden benefits, I think very few people continue to consider FBA after running these numbers.

I didn't. There was no chance I was going to make $5.76 off a $10 book, and put FBA out of my mind.

Fast forward six months. I was making a cross-country move that made transporting my Amazon inventory cost-prohibitive. Moving it myself would necessitate a U-Haul that would cost almost as much as the inventory was worth. The only option to even consider was shipping everything ahead via the post office's super-cheap Media Mail rate—an absolute logistical night-mare that would demand 150 boxes, thousands of feet in bubble wrap, and many days of work.

I stayed up all night, purchasing and reading every ebook available on FBA. At the time, this amounted to about 5 books.

What little literature there was forced my eyes open to FBA's game-changing advantages, the hidden benefits that left me shaking my head and wondering why I'd waited so long.

I shipped everything to FBA, repriced every item, and reworked my entire business architecture. And I made more in the first six months than I had made in the past two years *combined*.

THE FBA ADVANTAGE: TOP TEN LIST

These are the top ten advantages I learned of, which almost no one sees when giving a cursory look at FBA:

1. Selling at prices **way** above non-FBA sellers.
2. Instant approval to sell in categories non-FBA sellers have to apply for.
3. Access to an instant customer base of Amazon Prime customers, many

of whom will not purchase non-FBA offers.

4. Access to customers who use Amazon's free "Super Saver Shipping" option, for which only FBA offers qualify.

5. Instant "Featured Merchant" status, without which it is virtually impossible to sell in lucrative categories such as Grocery and Office Products.

6. Ability to price items at $3.99 more than non-FBA sellers, and still get the top spot on price results.

7. Outsourced shipping.

8. Outsourced customer service.

9. Leveraging the trust Amazon has built with Internet consumers over nearly 20 years. Although it's your product, customers know Amazon is doing the important work: shipping, packaging, and providing coverage under Amazon's customer service policies.

10. Effectively doubling your customer base: It is estimated that over 50% of Amazon customers have never purchased from a third party, non-FBA seller.

Of course, the first one is most important. Followed closely by the nine that follow.

Amazon built the trust. Amazon built their famed customer service reputation. Amazon spent years driving traffic to their site. And we get to take advantage of **all of it**—just by coming in at the last minute, giving all of our inventory to an Amazon warehouse, and giving them a somewhat larger cut of the sales price. We've done none of the work involved in building Amazon to where it is, but we get to take advantage of all of it. It almost seems unfair to Amazon.

There is no significant downside. Most people's first reaction to this is: "*Those extra fees are a pretty big downside.*" But they're not. Because those fees are usually more than offset by the higher price you can sell for having that "Fulfilled by Amazon" logo next to your products.

If you're thinking, "*I've never paid more for an item just because it has that logo,*" then you're not your own target market. You're not a Prime subscriber, and you don't ever spend more than $35 on Amazon to qualify for free shipping.

These are your customers:

- The Amazon buyer who has $29 worth of product in her cart and needs another $6 to get free shipping. She searches for a book that she doesn't want that bad, just to get that free shipping. Every used merchant-fulfilled copy is one cent ($4 with shipping), but she adds your $6 copy to her cart. She pays the extra $2 to save herself what would have been $10 in shipping. Win-win.

- The Amazon Prime subscriber who gets free second-day shipping and next-day shipping for only $3.99. He pays $99.99 a year for this service, and is going to get every penny out it. He'll only buy Prime-eligible products, for which only FBA and Amazon offers qualify. He clicks the "Prime Eligible" filtering tab when shopping and becomes the top listing. Yours is three times the price of the lowest non-FBA offer, but like most Amazon Prime members, he's willing to pay a premium to get the advantages of Prime. He wants the free shipping, and wants to know his purchase will get to him fast.

- The 50%+ of Amazon shoppers who have never bought from a non-FBA third party seller. These customers prefer to spend more to get the trust that comes with ordering from Amazon directly. A lot of people have been burned by non-FBA merchants who ship late, or not at all. Case in point: As I type this, I'm waiting for the clock to roll over to midnight so I'm able to file an A to Z Claim against a seller who never shipped a book I bought from him three weeks ago.

These are your new customers. And there are 50 million of them.

WHO ARE YOUR CUSTOMERS? THE FULL BREAKDOWN

Who is paying $9.99 for a book they could otherwise get for a penny plus postage? I'm going to reveal some of my personal sales statistics for some insight.

We can glean the motives of those who pay higher prices for FBA offers by looking at the shipping they chose. This information is available under the "Order" section of your seller's account. From this info, we can reasonably assume the following:

- Most who chose standard shipping are *non*-Prime subscribers who did so to qualify for free Super Saver Shipping.

- The vast, *vast* majority of those who chose second-day shipping are

Prime subscribers.

- And most who chose overnight shipping are Prime subscribers.

We know this because:

- Prime customers get free second-day shipping, so we can assume no one who chose standard shipping is a Prime subscriber. Following that, assuming your item was priced higher than a non-FBA competing listing, yours was probably chosen for the free shipping.

- Prime subscribers get free second-day shipping and overnight for $3.99, making it exceedingly likely that those who chose either of these options are Prime members.

I ran the numbers on my last month's sales. Here are the stats:

62% ordered second-day or overnight shipping.
38% ordered standard shipping.

That's approximately 62% of my customers who are Prime subscribers. This highlights my point that as an FBA seller, you should **not** price your items for the general Amazon buyer. Your market is largely Prime members. The rest are Amazon shoppers wanting free shipping. Price smartly and accordingly.

AMAZON PRIME: WHAT IS AMAZON PRIME?

Understanding Amazon Prime is central to success with FBA. Prime subscribers are the core of your business. Ignore this seemingly dry section at great risk to your entire financial future.

For $99.99 a year, Amazon's most loyal (and liberally spending) customers can enter into Amazon Prime, something that is seriously brilliant. Here is what they get:

- Free second-day shipping on all eligible offers (FBA and Amazon-direct offers only).
- $3.99 overnight shipping on the same.
- Free streaming on thousands of videos.
- Thousands of free books via the Kindle lending library.

As of late-2015, Amazon reported the number of Prime subscribers at 50 million. Every one of those customers is yours.

Amazon is secretive about exact details, but according to estimates Amazon Prime members:

- Increase their purchases on Amazon from $625 a year to $1,500 a year after they join.
- Spend 130% more than regular Amazon customers.
- May be responsible for as much as 20% of Amazon's overall sales in the U.S.

Additionally:

- 82% of them buy on Amazon even if the item is less expensive somewhere else.
- 92% of them plan to renew their membership.

Prime functions as sort of a loyalty oath, making Prime subscribers much less likely to search anywhere outside Amazon for a product. They are much more likely to begin and end their shopping with Amazon. And they are much more likely to purchase from FBA sellers. That's you.

And check this out: Amazon actually *loses* $11 per Prime subscriber, per year. This is consistent with Amazon's approach to win market share through profit-sucking deals, and make up for it on the back end—through customer loyalty, increased dollar-amount-per-purchase, and an increased number of purchases. And Prime subscribers deliver on all three.

To drive customers to Amazon Prime (and FBA purchases), Amazon has some interesting opt-in services.

The first is **Amazon Mom**—a free service that gives moms three free months of Amazon Prime (not sure how they verify "mom" status).

The second is **Amazon Student**—giving anyone with an ".edu" email address a Prime subscription free for six months, and $49.99 a year thereafter. This makes students a disproportionately higher percentage of Prime subscribers, and is one reason textbooks do so well for FBA sellers.

Both of these services drive large numbers of "regular" Amazon customers to Amazon Prime. These customers then become yours.

UNDERSTAND THE PRIME CUSTOMER: WHY THEY BUY

Let's take a walk through the mind of a Prime subscriber.

She wants a copy of *The Beastie Boys Anthology* photo book. A used copy is going for $8 from a merchant-fulfilled seller. As an FBA seller, you're offering it for $11.95.

All other things being equal (condition, etc.) you are guaranteed the sale. The Prime subscriber gets free second-day shipping for Amazon-fulfilled products, so there is literally zero incentive to go with the $8 item. In fact, there is a disincentive: She would have to pay postage of $3.99 on the $8 item, actually costing her slightly *more* than the Amazon-fulfilled offer. **And** she wouldn't receive second-day shipping. She'll go with the FBA seller every time.

Let's say the same book is going for $8 used and your FBA offer is increased to $15. You've priced your copy at nearly double the amount of the lowest non-FBA price. What will the Prime subscriber do?

She *could* go with the $8 copy. She'll pay $11.99 total (no free postage on non-FBA offers). She will then have to wait one to two weeks for the book, even though she has grown accustomed to second-day shipping. She also has no idea who is shipping the book, and is trusting a total stranger to deliver in a timely fashion. She is also at the mercy of that seller's return policy, and their willingness to comply if she wants to return the book.

And then there is the Prime service she pays $99 a year for—and the (perhaps subconscious) need to justify that expense, driving her toward Prime-eligible offers.

And she's likely to click the "FREE Super Saver Shipping offers only" button at the top, removing all merchant-fulfilled offers and showing her Prime-eligible offers only.

Her Prime subscription has already established her as a special kind of Amazon buyer. She has discretionary income to invest in membership, is willing to pay more for items to get the second-day shipping, and is spending literally over two times as much per year as the average non-Prime customer. She wants her book fast and is willing to pay more for this. And you're the only one who can deliver.

The sale is yours.

Prime Buyer Psychosis: A Case Study

Recently I was talking with a friend looking for a copy of a film I have a cameo in (don't ask). She told me she went to order a copy on Amazon, and though multiple copies were available, she didn't order because *"there were no Prime offers, so..."* She literally did not consider any non-Prime offer as an option, and the mindset was so deep-seated, she did not even feel obliged to explain. No Prime offer = no purchase. For many Prime subscribers, it's as simple as that.

FBA BY THE NUMBERS: EVERYTHING YOU WANT TO KNOW ABOUT THE MONEY

2

ALL FBA FEES EXPLAINED
THE 60% RULE
YOUR FBA SUPPORT STRUCTURE
AMAZON THE COMPANY: BY THE NUMBERS

FBA FEES: THE FULL STORY

This is what everyone wants to talk about—the money. How much is Amazon going to take from your used copy of *I Hope They Serve Beer in Hell?*

The short answer: About 40% of the sale price. More with lower-priced items, and less with higher. But on average, Amazon is going to take 40%.

Let's look at the fees when you sell a book:

FBA Advertised Fees (average fees for book fulfillment):

> 15% normal Amazon commission
> $1.02 "pick and pack" fee
> 55¢ fee per pound shipping fee
> $1.35 variable closing fee

The following "passive fees" also quietly nibble away at your profit:

> FBA labels (1¢ each)
> Shipping to UPS (Varies. 20-40¢ per book on average)
> Storage (1-2¢ per month)

This is all abstract, so in a moment we'll put this in real-world terms. First the "good news / bad news" about FBA fees…

GOOD NEWS / BAD NEWS

Bad News: The fees are brutal on lower end items, cutting your profit down by 50% or more.

Good News: Because FBA expands the number of profitable media items that you can sell tenfold, your increased inventory offsets the increased fees.

Bad News: See the first "Bad News."

Good News: You're not competing with everyone else, and you're not targeting every Amazon customer. You're competing with FBA sellers and targeting Amazon Prime subscribers—which allows you to charge at least $3.99 more than non-FBA offers, and often $7 to $10 (if not more) above non-FBA prices.

Bad News: You have to pay Amazon $1 to pack and ship every item.

Good News: You don't have to go to the post office. If you're anything like me, that's a relief—because you know those envelopes, tape, bubble wrap, and gas to the post office really add up. And don't forget that your time is worth something. Instead of spending hours packaging items and going to the post office, here's a smarter way to invest time in your business: go shopping for more inventory.

Bad News: Unlike merchant-fulfilled sales, you can't sell a book for a penny and still make $1.20 on postage.

Good News: That's not your business anymore. You're better than that.

Here's an analysis of some media items I sold through FBA recently. Let's look at sales price and fees versus the same sales and fees had I sold the items merchant-fulfilled.

Organic Gardening (book)
    Sold at $4.99
    Net FBA profit: $1.51
    Net MF profit: $4.08

Unstoppable Confidence (book)
    Sold at $9.99
    Net FBA profit: $5.76
    Net MF profit: $8.73

Hypnosis: A Comprehensive Guide (book)
    Sold at $14.99
    Net FBA profit: $9.64
    Net MF profit: $12.88

Lip Reading Made Easy (book)
    Sold at: $25.00
    Net FBA profit: $18.52
    Net MF profit: $21.49

Encyclopedia of Cryptozoology (book)
    Sold at $82.99
    Net FBA profit: $66.88
    Net MF profit: $73.18

American Dissidents (textbook)
    Sold at $125.00
    Net FBA profit: $104.69
    Net MF profit: $101.99

Works of Spike Jonze (DVD)
    Sold at $9.99
    Net FBA profit: $6.31
    Net MF profit: $8.67

Raw: Living Foods Diet (DVD)
    Sold at $40.00
    Net FBA Profit: $31.82
    Net MF Profit: $34.18

Spotlight by Outspoken (CD)
        Sold at $7.49
        Net FBA profit: $4.19
        Net MF profit: $6.85

Of course, these numbers are totally deceptive in terms of any real-world application. They assume that FBA and merchant-fulfilled offers will be selling at the same price. And they usually won't.

In every instance above, the sales price was $3.99 more than the lowest merchant-fulfilled offer ($3.99 is the shipping charge for books). Remember that you price with the assumption that the buyer will be using the free shipping option, so you can price at least the postage amount higher than merchant-fulfilled items and get the sale. You can also price above the lowest merchant-fulfilled price and still claim the coveted top spot in the listings. In any of the above examples, there is no way I could have received the same sales price without selling via FBA.

STEALING THE TOP SPOT

What do I mean by pricing $3.99 higher and still claiming the top spot? Check out this listing:

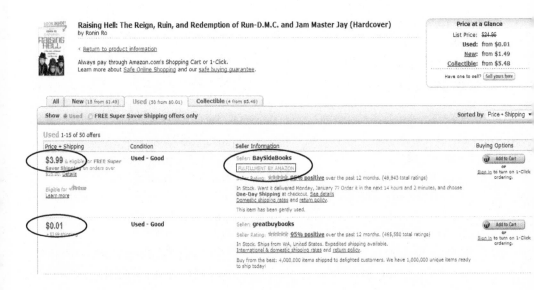

How does this happen? Because the positioning is based on price plus shipping. Amazon assumes the buyer will choose free shipping, so a book $3.99 higher is technically the cheapest option, and therefore gets top placement.

More money and better placement. Win-win.

RUNNING YOUR OWN NUMBERS

Amazon has an FBA Revenue Calculator where you can plug in any item on Amazon and see your net profit vs. the same item sold merchant-fulfilled (MF).

Run your own numbers at: *sellercentral.amazon.com/gp/fbacalc/fba-calculator.html*.

amazon services
seller central

Fulfillment by Amazon Revenue Calculator (Beta)

Provide your fulfillment costs and see real-time cost comparisons between your fulfillment and our offering for customer orders fulfilled on Amazon.com.

Disclaimer - This Fulfillment by Amazon Revenue Calculator should be used as a guide in evaluating FBA only. Amazon does not warrant the accuracy of the information or calculations in this Fulfillment by Amazon Revenue Calculator. Independent analysis of the output of this Fulfillment by Amazon Revenue Calculator should be conducted to verify the results. Please consult the Amazon Services Business Solutions Agreement for up-to-date costs and fees.

Skeletons of the Prairie: Abandoned Rural Codington County, South Dakota [Hardcover]
ASIN: 1578641063
Product Dimensions: 11 x 8.75 x 0.75 inches
Shipping Weight: 2.35 pounds

See Product Details

🔵 Try another product

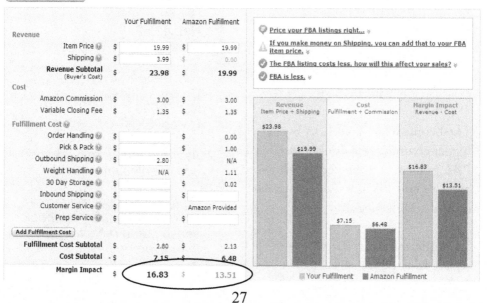

THE 60% RULE

Look at my own Amazon disbursements (see sidebar) to get a clear example of the 60% rule.

In the sidebar, you'll see a breakdown of my gross sales versus take-home profit over the last seven payment periods (every payment represents two weeks of sales). *Note: These seven deposits cover a textbook season, so these numbers are a little higher than average.*

You can see from these numbers that Amazon fees take up approximately 40% of the sales total. This will vary based on number of units, size of products, etc.

When sourcing inventory, always defer to the net payout field of your scouting app for the exact number. But when you need to do some analog math, expect to take home 60% of the final sale price.

STORAGE FEES: TOO SMALL TO SEE, TOO LOW TO MATTER

Like amoeba, when something is so small you can't see it, it may as well not exist. So it is with FBA storage fees.

The people who avoid FBA because of bigger commissions don't understand FBA pricing, and the people who complain about FBA storage fees have never looked at those fees.

The official fee calculation is 48¢ per square foot, per month.

My last seven Amazon deposits

(Two weeks per pay period)

Pay Period One
Gross: 6,178.52
Net: 3,918
I keep: 63%

Pay Period Two
Gross: 5,898
Net: 3,462
I keep: 62%

Pay Period Three
Gross: 5,692
Net: 3,532
I keep: 62%

Pay Period Four
Gross: 6,764
Net: 4,034
I keep: 60%

Pay Period Five
Gross: 7,792
Net: 4,556
I keep: 58%

Pay Period Six
Gross: 7,386
Net: 4,252
I keep: 58%

Pay Period Seven
Gross: 10,844
Net: 7,036
I keep: 65%

Average take-home percentage of sales price: 61%.

(This period covered the holidays + January textbook season, and reflect higher than average payouts)

28

What this translates to in useful terms is this (on average):

$.01 per month for a trade paperback (or 14¢ a year).
$.03 per month for a textbook (or 45¢ a year).
$.01 per month for a DVD (or 9¢ a year).
Less than $.01 month for a CD (or 5¢ a year).

Note: storage fees increase during the holidays (October to December) from 48¢ per cubic foot to 64¢.

You can store one of the largest textbooks known to man for 7¢ a month. Storage fees should be no factor at all, considering the enormous sales leverage you obtain from FBA. If 14¢ per year is the deal-breaker making an otherwise profitable item unprofitable, you shouldn't be selling that item. Your margins are just too low.

After fees, 1¢ per month on a $3.99 book that I'll sit on for a year will eventually eat 20% of the profit margin, but that's a book I never should have sent to Amazon. The only time I'll allow a book like that into my inventory is when I've purchased a bulk lot and the book is in my house already. And only then if I know that book is going to convert quickly.

You might say: "Sixty cents is sixty cents. It only takes me 20 seconds to scan and label a book." Yet with anything, there are hidden costs.

Consider the psychic impact of running a business in which you sell fifty units a day, and go to sleep with a daily income of... $28. Does this create an inspired, motivated entrepreneur? Does this generate zeal for your business and make you wake up charged to do it again another day?

It doesn't. It drains morale. It kills your spirit. Where there is little reward, there is little enthusiasm. It is not a sustainable model. You get from the universe what you ask of it. Take your eyes off the pennies, and you'll start to see dollars.

If you can accept that you must spend money to make money, FBA storage fees are one of the better returns you can get on any investment. Instead of looking at storage as a sunk cost, focus on the tremendous value you receive: using someone's warehouse for storage and freeing up that space in your home. Or, if your inventory is big enough, saving you rental fees on your own warehouse space. And this doesn't even touch the other benefits Amazon is offering. It is an incredible value.

EVERY OTHER FBA FEE EXPLAINED

Long-Term Storage Fees

This part shouldn't be confusing, but to a lot of sellers, it is.

There is an extra fee charged every six months if these two factors are in place:
  1. You have more than one copy of any item, and;
  2. You have it in storage for more than six months.

For all items that qualify, every six months you will be charged $11.25 a cubic foot for any item at a warehouse longer than six months, and $22.50 a cubic foot for any item at a warehouse longer than a year.

This is what the fees look like for common items:

> DVD: 70¢
> Average paperback: $1.10
> CD: 15¢

That is the amount you will be charged every six months for each item *over* the first one.

The first item in any SKU is excluded from the fee. You get a lifetime of storage for that one item for the same negligible monthly fee.

Amazon doesn't want lazy sellers and remainder book behemoths to use their warehouses as cheap storage space for books they know they'll never sell. Long-term storage fees are a way to force every seller to ask this question before sending a shipment with multiples: *Do I think these will sell in the next six months?*

Oversize fee

Amazon has special "pick and pack fees" for exceptionally large items. They vary, but these are the fee-tiers: $4.03, $5.07, $8.12, and $10.25, depending on the size.

This is a serious consideration for some larger books, toys, sporting goods, etc. I had a half-dozen baby stroller covers in stock when the first oversize fees went into effect, and it cut my profits down on each by over 50%.

Remember this: High margins = the luxury of not caring about fees.

Amazon switches up fees and commissions all the time. The good news is that if you keep your margins high on everything, and don't become a book-selling bottom-feeder, nothing Amazon is going to do will make you wince. You've already buffered yourself from Amazon's next curveball by building the potential for new threats into your margins.

KEEPING THE PIRATE SHIP AFLOAT: YOUR FBA SUPPORT STRUCTURE

Your new empire is not the kind that requires aggressive diplomacy or quelling uprisings with force or propaganda. Your empire is a benign rule with an army of one that requires you merely to throw money at obstacles and watch them vanish. Grown-ups call this "overhead." Here's the monthly cost breakdown:

Unlimited data cell plan: You may already have this, but I pay $30 more than I otherwise would, so I consider it a business expense.

Storage fees: Very roughly, $6 per month per 500 books. (Prices increase during holidays).

Scanning app & listing program: $70 per month for the package I use (FBA Scan app + ScanPower listing program).

Packing tape and labels: I use dollar store tape and buy labels on eBay at about $10 for 1000. We'll assume you're using ten rolls of tape per month and sending in 500 books.

Amazon Pro-Merchant account: With a Pro-Merchant account, Amazon waives the 99¢ closing fee per item. If you sell more than 40 items per month, this saves you money. It would cost you more to *not* have it, so this is not really an expense (I'm not going to include it in the final tally).

Internet at your home: $50 (another one you probably pay for already).

Shipping for 500 items: We'll say $125, average.

Total: $280

To keep the ship afloat every month, you're going to be spending approximately $280. Can you afford it? You can't not afford it.

AMAZON, THE COMPANY: BY THE NUMBERS

Amazon, formerly called "the biggest bookstore on earth," is now just "the biggest store on earth."

To understand how powerful FBA is, you must understand what a behemoth Amazon itself is:

- Amazon put the entire Borders book chain out of business.
- Amazon is threatening the demise of Barnes & Noble, which has been in business since 1917.
- n 2015, Amazon surpassed Walmart as the most valuable retailer in the United States
- Amazon has 300 million customers each month.
- Amazon's current annual revenue from book sales is $5.25 billion.
- Amazon has a 20% share of total e-commerce traffic.
- Amazon sells over 100 million books per year.
- FBA was credited with being a "key driver in eBay's recent poor performance".
- Amazon has a market value of $247 billion, which is about equal to that of Best Buy, Staples, Target, Sears, JC Penney, Macy's, Nordstrom, and Kohl's *combined.*

THE AMAZON CUSTOMER

Who are Amazon's (soon to be your) customers?

- 25% are over the age of 50.
- More than half earn $60,000 year or more.

There is no information available on the demographic makeup of Prime subscribers. Because of the $99 subscription fee, and the program catering to consumers who value good service and shipping speed over getting the lowest price, we can assume their average income is well over that of the average Amazon customer. And more discretionary income equals looser spending habits.

More numbers

Look at these revenue numbers for the two major bookselling channels in 2014:

> Amazon Media (books, music, movies): $11 billion
> Barnes and Noble: $6.38 billion

At the end of 2014, Amazon MarketPlace (aka "third party" sellers — that's you) reached 40% of Amazon sales volume, putting the units sold by these sellers in the hundreds of millions.

Under the mantra of "get big fast," Jeff Bezos launched Amazon into a hyperdrive acceleration of growth by losing money on nearly everything in order to capture market share. They've survived the dot-com bubble explosion and gobbled up that market share by selling almost everything at a loss — shipping, bestselling books, everything — and making it up down the road through customers who spend more and return often. This forward-thinking, counterintuitive model has lead to the Amazon we have today: "the biggest store in the world."

THE BIG ONE

And here is perhaps the most telling — and important — statistic of all. At the time of this writing:

44% of consumers began their product research on Amazon, 21% began their product research on a search engine.

This is big. Online shopping doesn't start on Google anymore. People go to Amazon.

This essentially means you are getting the best SEO in the world — for free. It's actually more effective than paid search engine marketing such as Adwords. More than double your customers are probably doing a product search on Amazon before Google. The implications of this are huge.

If you have either the lowest price or the most appealing overall Amazon offer for any product in the world, the next time anyone in the entire country wants that product you have a better chance of getting that sale than *any other single person.*

Having that offer on Amazon is like having the first thing people see when they walk into the most popular store in the world.

With Amazon and FBA, everything is taken care of: massive traffic, massive SEO, outsourced customer service, and outsourced shipping. So you're only left with one job:

Getting inventory.

ARCHITECTURE OF AN FBA EMPIRE

3

THE EQUIPMENT
THE SOFTWARE
BOOTSTRAPPING ALL OF IT

AWESOME ARCHITECTURE: EQUIPMENT FOR YOUR FBA EMPIRE

When I finally committed to make the switch to FBA, I didn't cut corners on equipment. I upgraded to a mid-range Android phone, Scanfob scanner, the full scanning app / listing software package, and a Dymo label printer. Total start-up costs were approximately $650 out of the gate.

With the buying power that a high-powered scanning app & scanner gave me, I think I made that back in three days.

Here is the structural support for your FBA empire:

- Scanfob barcode scanner: $300 (*serialio.com*)
- Dymo label printer: $80 on eBay
- Labels: $10 for 1000
- Smart phone: $200
- Scanning app: $30 per month (I use FBA Scan, but cheaper apps are also available)
- Unlimited data plan: Approximately $30 more than standard service

BOOTSTRAPPING

There is another way to start: invest minimally in equipment. Use the camera function of your phone to scan barcodes or manually enter ISBNs. Print labels on sheets instead of buying a label printer.

This is an option, but all good equipment is going to pay for itself. It will cost you more to *not* buy it. Which is the case for everything I'm describing here.

If a $650 investment is not an option, here are ways to cut that back:

If you already have an Android phone, reduce your cost by $200.

If you buy a cheaper Android, reduce your cost by $100. (You will give up screen size and speed.)

If you don't buy a Dymo label printer, reduce your cost by $80.

I purchased a used Dymo for $55 plus shipping on eBay. Without one, you still have the option of printing labels on sheets from the Amazon interface. Assuming a major reason you're doing FBA is to streamline your business, be warned that hunting and pecking through stacks of books to label them one at a time is not in harmony with your streamlining objectives. It's a time-drainer.

And take note that to operate without a label printer, you'll still need a regular, desktop one.

If you purchase a used Scanfob or cheaper brand barcode scanner, reduce your cost by $200.

The Scanfob is an elegant micro-sized scanner that I would sooner get a face tattoo than do business without. Its chief benefits are size and stealth. There are too many places where scanning flamboyantly compromises your short and long terms goals as a bookseller. You're inviting competition from passersby and confrontation from store owners. The Scanfob is the size of a small box of matches.

If you just can't spend $300 that you'll make back in two days anyway, there are other options. The most popular alternative, as far as I can tell, is the Unitech MS910 Handheld Barcode Scanner. As of this writing, it's $125 on Amazon. I haven't used it and can't comment, but it is also wireless, and appears to give the Scanfob a run for its money.

You may be able to get something compatible that will cost as little as $100 used. Consider both the obvious and hidden costs of working with unsightly, unwieldy, substandard equipment before investing in anything.

If you forgo purchasing a scanner and use your phone's camera, reduce your cost by $300.

Many apps allow you to use your phone's camera to "scan" barcodes. This is a less nimble method that will cut down your speed significantly when you're in the field.

If you forgo the use of listing software, reduce your cost by $40

(and $40 every month thereafter)

You will process all your listing and shipments directly though Amazon. It slows the work flow, yet is an option.

If you use a one-time purchase canning app like Profit Bandit, reduce your monthly costs by $10+.

This won't reduce your startup costs, yet will save you money in the long term.

CELL SIGNAL STRENGTH: THE WEAK LINK

I won't go into phone options (there are thousands of them) except to say that the two FBA scouting apps I've used (ScanPower and FBA Scan) only work on iPhones or Android-based phones. So you have to start with one of those.

With cell-signal-based apps like ScanPower, the phone you're using is less the issue than the strength of your provider's service. This is a big one, because it all comes down to the range and strength of service. Where there is weak service, you're out of business. I do not recommend cell-service-based apps.

The deeper inside the building the books are, and the more fortified the walls, the more likely you'll have to wait long periods between scans. When I was using cell-based apps, there were stores which were goldmines for me, but going through them thoroughly took half a day because I literally had to pull books I suspected had value from the shelves until my cart was full, then roll them fifty yards to the front of the store just to get enough service to scan. After scanning every book, I rolled them to the back, reshelved the valueless books, and refilled my cart. Repeat fifty times, and you have just described how I spent several days each month.

The question *not* to ask is "*Have I ever experienced a dropped call with this provider?*" Scanning a barcode is a more data-heavy transaction, and most places I've been where scan results don't load, I can still get a call out.

Instead, go to every place you intend to source inventory and look solely at the number of bars indicating your signal strength. A weak signal can cause pages to take twenty seconds or more to load. If you don't have more than half your bars, you may want a different provider.

I strongly recommend a local database-based app like FBA Scan. This allows you to download Amazon's database directly into your phone, and bring up results instantly—no cell service required.

Backup: Amazon Shopping app

This free app allows you to take a photo of any book cover and get instant Amazon data on that item. The app's ability to read the image and match it to the corresponding book is pretty remarkable, and it has no trouble with weird angles or intruding fingers.

I like to have this as backup for situations other apps just can't handle. Primarily, this means books with no ISBN, or where barcodes are covered with price stickers. (Major downside: the Amazon app won't show you sales rank.)

SET UP A SELLERS ACCOUNT

Now that you have your equipment, it's time to set up an account to sell on Amazon. I won't even walk you through this—it's too boring. The only thing I'll weigh in on here is the free account, versus Professional…

Individual vs. Professional accounts

You're starting out and FBA is still an experiment. The question is: Do you sign up for a $40 per month Professional account, or keep the free, "Individual" plan?

This isn't a big question. If you are starting with a level of inventory from which you can expect to sell (not list – *sell*) forty items a month, then it will cost more to *not* have a Professional account. The chief benefit is the 99¢ fee that is waived from every sale.

If you're unsure whether you'll be selling forty items your first month (or any month thereafter), here is a breakdown of the benefits and detriments of each plan:

Selling Plan Features	Professional (Pro Merchant Subscription)	Individual (Sell Your Stuff)
Best for Sellers who..	Plan on selling more than 40 items a month	Plan on selling fewer than 40 items a month
Monthly subscription fee	$ 39.99	N/A
Per-item closing fee	referral fee & variable closing fee	$0.99 + referral fee & variable closing fee
Ability to create new products and add them to the Amazon catalog	✓	X
Use of feeds, spreadsheets, and other tools to load inventory	✓	X
Access to order reports and order-related feeds	✓	X
Amazon-set shipping rates for Books, Music, Video and DVD products	✓	✓
Seller-customized shipping rates (For products other than Books, Music, Video and DVD products)	✓	X
Promotions, Gift Services, and other special listing features	✓ 1	X
Eligible for featured seller status; this is necessary to win the Buy Box on product detail pages	✓ 1	X
Listings automatically expire after 60 days	X	✓

*The ability to collect US sales and use taxes on your orders
[1] does not apply to Books, Music, Video and DVD products

LONE WOLF BOOKSELLING: SOME BACKGROUND

There was a time someone had to have a deep knowledge of books and be able to know at a glance if a book had value. They purchased based on this knowledge, and — because no brain can store data for 10 million books — intuition. Those who had the broadest knowledge of books won the race.

Old.   Older.

Then came the first wave of Internet-capable cell phones. Sharp resellers could go anywhere used books were sold, type ISBNs into Amazon or Abe.com, and make a buying decision. Suddenly the tech savvy buyers had a huge advantage over those who had spent a lifetime dealing in used books.

Then came the barcode scanners. Programs like A Seller Tool debuted, allowing sellers to download Amazon's media database into a PDA, then uti-

lize a barcode scanner to scan the barcodes of media items (books, music, & DVDs) and get instant data on the item's sales rank and value. This was a big development.

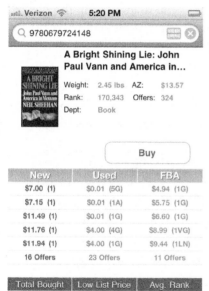

Barcode scanning ability was a huge advantage, but all programs had a major blindspot: none displayed FBA seller competition. Since FBA sellers generally don't consider merchant fulfilled offers competition, these programs left sellers to hazard a guess as to an item's FBA value.

Then, in 2010, came the first FBA scanning apps. They were the first programs to put center-stage the info that matters most: Your FBA competition.

With this, a spotlight was flipped on. And it shone directly on the profit.

But the glory days were short lived.

A short 2 years later, in 2012, Amazon changed everything, and stopped sharing most FBA data with third-party apps. One dark day in September, the FBA column in our scanning apps went (mostly) blank.

Why did Amazon decide they didn't want us to have FBA data? The short explanation is that Amazon wants to force prices down, and for FBA sellers to compete with merchant fulfilled offers only - not FBA.

It's not quite as bad as it sounds, and FBA sellers can still get this data. It just takes slightly more work. More on this later.

THE NEW GENERATION OF SCANNING APPS

These next-generation apps have been accurately likened to a set of goggles that lets you walk into a store and only see the items worth money.

Why an FBA-specific scanning app? Booksellers using FBA have a special set of guidelines for buying and selling. As stated, number one is that (for most items) they are not competing against non-FBA sellers (aka "merchant fulfilled," or MF). This means that MF prices for books and media are of little relevance. The reason being that when you're targeting Prime subscribers and buyers wanting free "Super Saver" shipping, you're leveraging the power of those services to give you an advantage much more important than "the cheapest price."

Starting with ScanPower, a new generation of scanning apps emerged. FBA Scan, Profit Bandit, Scout Rabbit, Neatoscan, and Scout Pal all rose up to serve the FBA seller, giving the information we need to make a buying decision.

Just as cool, some apps (FBA Scan and ScanPower being two) break down your net profit, showing exactly how much money will go in your pocket when all the smoke clears. They factor in all FBA fees (including weight of the item) and give you the number that really matters: your profit.

A blindspot of the old generation of apps was that few allowed you to scan non-media categories like Office Products or Lawn and Patio. While books and media may be the easiest category to source in, it is not always the most profitable. FBA Scan and others from the new crop give you info on every single item in Amazon's catalog.

After being weaned on ScanPower, I made the switch to FBA Scan, and have found it far superior. It offers all the same crucial features, as well as not requiring a cell signal *and* returning results instantly. In my opinion, it has far exceeded ScanPower and become my preferred app.

To ensure this book is not obsolete by the time it is in your hands, I will give a list of the crucial features an FBA seller will want in *any* FBA scouting service rather than focus on one program (FBA Scan is currently the only app I know of to offer all of these):

- **Sales prices that include postage**: Your program should add postage to the selling price, because most of your customers are going to be choosing free shipping. This allows you to add the cost of postage to the price and still claim the top spot in the listings.

- **FBA competition**: As we'll cover, Amazon limits how much of this we can see, but whatever they *do* share, the app should display.

- **Net profit**: The only figure that really matters.

- **Product image**: So you can see what the Amazon customer sees, making sure your item matches the Amazon listing.

- **Sales rank**: The top piece of information you need to safely answer the question: *Will this sell?*

- **Sales rank history:** This is extremely valuable, allowing you to know what demand for an item is across a given period of time - not just the moment you scan.

- **Link to the Amazon product page**: Very important to get more info if the data provided isn't sufficient. For example, you need to know if the barcode you scanned is for a set, or one book. You should have the option to click through to Amazon and see exactly what the buyer will see.

- **Sales category**: Because a 100,000 rank in Books means something entirely different than in Tools.

- **Amazon's selling price**: Sometimes this price is lower than every other seller's price. While it could change, ultimately this is the one price you can't ever beat.

- **Data for non-media items (grocery, toys, health & beauty — everything)**: While reselling non-media items is outside the scope of this book, other categories have huge potential for profit.

- **Volume of inventory for competing FBA sellers**: If you're buying based on a strategy of pricing your item second-highest and waiting for the lowest offer to sell, you'll want to know if one item needs to sell—or 100 of them do—before you make money.

- **Prices for non-FBA offers**: If there are no other FBA sellers offering your product, **and** the item is not ranked incredibly well (for example, by my criteria, worse than 1 million in books), you'll want to consider prices set by non-FBA sellers when setting your price. The book just may not be selling often enough to get away with a price $10 or more above the lowest non-FBA seller. Whatever sales rank threshold you set, there will be a point where you base your price solely on non-FBA sellers, and you'll need the data to make that decision.

SCANNING: THE MECHANICS

For an FBA business, this is where the rubber meets the road. It all comes down to the laser from your scanner hitting a barcode. From books, CDs, DVDs, and onward to non-media items — from natural dishwashing detergent to cases of glow sticks (two purchases I made today).

How does it work?

1. Scan an item's barcode.
2. Interpret the results that display on your screen.

Let's back up: You have your barcode scanner. You have an iPhone or Android device. And you signed up for your free trial of FBA Scan. It's Saturday

Amazon Autopilot

morning and you're at your first garage sale, ready to see if there is profit in this, or just a lot of hype.

The first part is easy: hit the button, scan the barcode, and the corresponding info shows up on your app.

The second part is what most people get wrong. Making the decision to buy is a calculation based on at least six pieces of information. Knowing how to read that information to make an intelligent buying decision is where most make their mistake.

When you scan an item's barcode, your program (in my case, FBA Scan) should show the following information:

- Sales rank
- Sales rank history
- Department
- Amazon's sale price
- Number of offers new and used (if applicable)
- Number of FBA offers (if applicable)
- Number of items in inventory for each offer
- Net profit

This is the information you need to make a sound decision and why it matters:

Sales rank
Know how to interpret a sales rank in every category. In a later chapter, I include a cheat sheet which gives the sales rank that make up the top 1%, 5%, and 15% in every category.

Department
Know what the selling restrictions are for each category, specifically which categories allow you to sell used products, which allow only new, and which require approval in before selling.

Amazon's sale price
Easy to overlook, this price is important because it can fluctuate, at times leaving every FBA offer higher than Amazon's price. Amazon's price is always the ceiling. You cannot, and should not try to, compete with Amazon.

Merchant fulfilled offers

While I've stated often that FBA sellers are only competing against other FBA offers, there is a point where FBA offers can be so high that they will lose all potential customers to merchant fulfilled offers. If a book is $4.99 MF, and the lowest FBA offer is $39.99, you will usually have trouble competing at that price (unless it's a well-ranked textbook). You will need the MF price as a starting point to determine a competitive price point for your FBA offer.

Number of FBA offers

Important to gauge your competition.

Inventory number for each offer

If your strategy is to price higher than the lowest FBA offer and wait for the lowest to sell out, this number is important to determine how long you'll be waiting.

UNDERSTANDING SCANNING APP BLINDSPOTS

Amazon severely restricts the FBA data scanning apps can display. Bottom line: Your app will *not* show you other FBA offers unless they're lowball offers. What does this mean? Here are the hard facts:

Your scanning app will only display an FBA offer *if it is priced in the lowest 20 of its condition category* (either New or Used). Anything else will not be displayed.

So if I advocate only pricing against other FBA offers, how do you get this data? Two ways: Clicking through to Amazon, and "reading between the lines."

Clicking through: Any self-respecting FBA scanning app should offer a link to view a product directly on Amazon. And not a just a link to the product page - a link to the offers, filtered to show FBA offers only. Amazon will never be able to take this away. This gets you the most accurate data. It also takes a lot of time.

"Reading between the lines": This is considerably more advanced and complex. The idea is this:

There is a predictable ratio of FBA offers to merchant fulfilled offers at various sales rank's. When you know these ratios, you can "read between the lines" of your scanning app data, and determine the likely volume of FBA competition – *even though your scanning app won't show it to you.*

Let's say you see a book ranked 250,000, with 200 non-FBA ("merchant ful-filled") offers, showing no FBA offers on your app. Those skilled in "reading between the lines" know this is a book to avoid. The visible data points indicate those FBA offers are there, probably in the $4.01 to $5 range.

Let's say you see a book ranked 5,000, with 30 non-FBA offers, showing no FBA offers. Those skilled in "reading betweent the lines" would buy this up instantly. The data indicates there probably aren't any FBA offers, and you can price your FBA offer (almost) as high as you want and still get a sale.

This skill takes a little time to learn, but pay attention to the data, and those ratios, and you'll pick it up quickly. And it will save you a massive amount of time from no longer having to click over to Amazon to confirm FBA offers.

(I offer a full, detailed tutorial on this Jedi tactic in my article *"The Penny Book Profit Formula"* on FBAmastery.com.)

STREAMLINING THE LISTING PROCESS WITH SCANPOWER

As of this writing, ScanPower's listing program is $40 a month. The Scan-Power listing tool is an online interface that dramatically simplifies the process of listing your products on Amazon. There are other desktop appli-cations that perform the same function, but I will focus here on ScanPower because it is what I know.

Let's say you're shipping off 100 books. Here's how you have to do it without listing software:

1. List your book by entering the ISBN or UPC manually into Amazon.
2. Print a sheet or sheets of barcode labels.
3. Peel off each label one at a time, hunt through every one of your 100 books until you find the corresponding item, and apply the label.
4. Repeat x100.

(To be fair, if you have a label printer and scanner Amazon offers a barely less annoying "Scan and Ship" feature.)

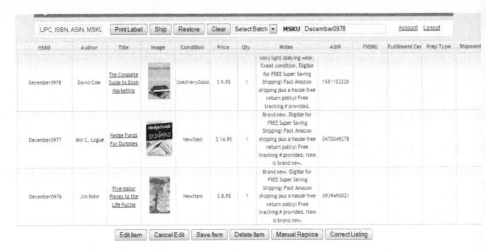

Either way, it's a project-and-a-half.

Let's do the same process with listing software:

1. Scan item.
2. Your item page will load. Choose the condition and set the price (sales rank & competing prices are shown in real time).
3. Print label & affix it to the product right then.
4. Repeat x100.

These software solutions are browser-based, and the appeal is that you do each step without ever leaving the page. Only when every book is scanned in do you hit the "ship" button and cleanly upload the entire shipment to Amazon. You will then finish the last few steps of the process (setting the weight and printing box labels) from your Amazon seller's account.

The second appeal of listing applications is that you only touch the book once. You pick it up, scan it, label it, and put it directly into a box to be shipped. Done.

Doing it via Amazon's way, you would pick up the book, list it, and then pick it up again later to label and box it.

When you're dealing in volume, the time-saving advantage of listing software is huge.

FBA BUYING STRATEGY: WHEN TO BUY, WHEN TO PASS

4

BUYING STRATEGY IS EVERYTHING
CRACKING THE SALES RANK CODE
SALES RANK CHEAT SHEET FOR EVERY CATEGORY
LONG TAIL THEORY
THE LONG TAIL TEST
USING PAID APPS TO MAKE BUYING DECISIONS

INTELLIGENT BUYING STRATEGY

Aim for the "3x rule" — for every $1 you invest, you want at least $3 back.

With some exceptions for very well-ranked items, I won't buy anything I can't triple my money on, with a minimum profit threshold of $3. My rigid buying parameters prevent hundreds of brief moments throughout the day where I stop and ask, *Should I buy?*

I know the cost of the book and I know my net payout (displayed by your scanning app). So when I'm buying, I become a machine. I know if I'm paying $1 for a book, and I see a $3 payout somewhere in my future, it's mine. If a book is ranked well enough, the price I set doesn't even need to be in the top two lowest FBA offers, but I would like to see it in the top three to know my investment is coming back to me threefold in short time.

There are always exceptions. I wouldn't pass on doubling my money if the rank was high or the net profit was high enough. I haven't hesitated to spend $20 on books that I know will bring $40 back to me in short time.

You may have a different profit-tolerance. You may be content doubling your money. You may operate by a "5x Rule." Having a formula is what's important. Without it, you weigh yourself down in hundreds of tiny moments of indecision throughout a day. Know how much you're paying, how much profit you need to see from each item, and go on autopilot.

FBA is best viewed as a money making machine: For every $10 you put in, you should be getting $30 or more back. The more money you feed it, the more you get back. If the inventory you're bringing in always outpaces your sales by a certain percent — with the better ranking books always flying out the door and the riskier, long tail books biding their time — then you have a snowball effect in motion, and your Amazon payments will grow and grow.

MY EVOLUTION OF BUYING LOW AND SELLING HIGH

I started out as a merchant-fulfilled seller with limited capital. Amazon was untested for me and I wanted to see results before throwing money at something that may not throw it back for a while, if ever. I purchased very conservatively, only buying books ranked better than 250,000 that I could make $10 or more dollars on.

This limited my inventory options dramatically, but I remained risk-averse until the model began to prove itself.

As my comfort with Amazon grew, I loosened my standards. I became more comfortable with books ranked up to 500,000 and with lower margins.

And so on. All the while, I was feeding profits back into the machine. Buying riskier bulk lots. Focusing on volume. Relaxing my need for immediate returns. Buying more and watching the results.

When my inventory hit about 1,500, I had outgrown the self-fulfillment model and moved all my inventory over to FBA. Suddenly the percentage of books that were profitable increased literally tenfold. My inventory ballooned, and so did my sales.

CRACKING THE CODE: WHAT IS SALES RANK?

There is a magic number that we live and die by called *sales rank*.

For every category (excluding, for some reason, many consumer electronics items), there is a number in the product description that aims to capture an item's popularity.

Amazon does not disclose their algorithm that determines sales rank. This chapter will be my attempt to pool all the available info to help us determine how to interpret that number. And it's an important one.

Product Details

Hardcover: 465 pages
Publisher: Harpercollins; 1st edition (September 1992)
Language: English
ISBN-10: 0060167548
ISBN-13: 978-0060167547
Product Dimensions: 9.1 x 6.4 x 1.6 inches
Shipping Weight: 1.9 pounds
Average Customer Review: ★★★★☆ (12 customer reviews)
Amazon Best Sellers Rank: #1,272,208 in Books (See Top 100 in Books)

Would you like to update product info, give feedback on images, or tell us about a lower price?

There is debate about how much sales rank should factor into a buying decision. On one end, those who say that the only thing that matters is your profit margin, meaning if a book costs 25¢ and it's going for $25 on Amazon, they're buying it — even if the sales rank indicates it hasn't sold a copy in five years. On the other end are those who need solid proof a book is in heavy demand before they're spending one cent, no matter if a book is selling on Amazon for $500.

Of course, Amazon calculates sales rank through a complicated formula we can only speculate on. Understanding how sales rank works – what it is, and what it is not – is very important to the Amazon seller. So I'm going to sum up everything as I understand it in one sentence.

Amazon Sales Rank is defined as: *The period of time since an item last sold.*

That's it. It sounds too simple, but it's all you have to remember.

Starting from one hour after a book sells, its rank will start to drift up (to a higher number) until it sells again. The longer the gap between sales, the further its sales rank slips and the higher the number goes. And when the book sells again, it will jump back down and start the upwards journey once more.

I'm in somewhat of a privileged position to know how sales rank works. One of my side businesses is publishing; I have ten books in print at the moment. All my titles are on Amazon, so I can see when a book sells, and precisely what one sale does to sales rank. Here's what I've learned:

A single sale will cause any book to jump to a sales rank of approximately 100,000. Maybe 70,000, maybe 120,000. Two sales in a day will bring it up to around 30,000. The actual rank can be on either end of these estimates, depending on how many other books have sold that day on Amazon.

None of my books sell well enough for me to be able to offer personal testimony beyond what two copies sold in a day translates to. But the available info says that a book ranked steadily at 5,000 is selling about 11 copies per day. A book with a steady rank of 100,000 is averaging a little more than one copy sold per day.

After a sale, a book will hold that sales rank for one hour – Amazon calculates sales rank every hour. And then, the rank starts its upward decline. If no other copies sell, the next day the rank will be approximately 250,000. After two days, the rank will hit somewhere around 380,000 (again, ballpark figures here).

Watching this with my own eyes was a seismic reality check. For the first two years of selling on Amazon, I considered anything beyond 500,000 to be the black abyss of sales which books would disappear into and never been seen again. Finding out a book at 500,000 sold *three days ago* was mind blowing. Actually, when I learned this all I did was run the rough math on how many tens of thousands of dollars in sales I'd lost out on because I never took the time to understand what sales rank was.

Most Amazon sellers still believe in this abyss, and put it somewhere around 1 million. If 500,000 means that a book sold three days ago, what does 1 million mean? Keep in mind almost none of the Amazon gurus will advise you to buy books ranked worse than 1 million. Let's take a closer look. How long ago did a book ranked 1 million sell?

Have a seat.

A book ranked 1 million sold about ten days ago. That's it.

Picture holding two books. According to your scanner, the book in your right hand has a rank of 100,000. The book in your left, a rank of 800,000. Both will cost you 50¢, and sell on Amazon for $10. Most sellers would run to the counter with the 100,000-ranked book. Most would pass on the 800,000-ranked book. But the only thing that separates them is about *seven days*.

The folly here is that there is no such thing as "a book ranked 100,000" or "a book ranked 800,000." There are only books with those ranks *at that moment*. That 100,000 book could be 800,000 in a week. And that 800,000 book could be 100,000 in five minutes. Sales rank only tells you one thing: How long it's been since the last copy sold.

Being the 1 millionth bestselling book anywhere doesn't sound like an achievement. But Amazon does such huge volume that 1 million isn't bad in a bookstore that is selling almost 275,000 books per day.

Here are a couple of takes on what sales rank converts to in actual sales, starting with a sales rank of 1 selling approximately 10,000 copies a day.

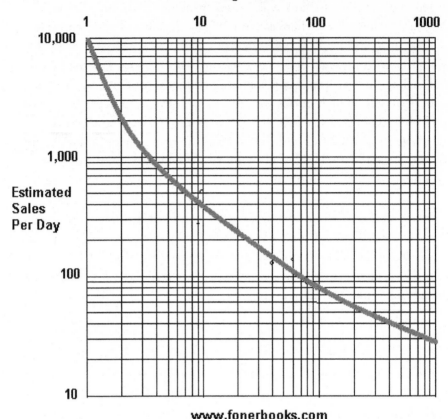

Average Sales Rank

www.fonerbooks.com

Sales rank of 1: 10,000 copies per day.
Sales rank 10: 400 copies per day.
Sales rank of 100: 70 copies per day.
Sales rank of 1,000: 30 copies per day.
Sales rank of 5,000: 80 copies per week.
Sales rank of 10,000: 60 copies per week.
Sales rank of 100,000: 10 copies per week.
Sales rank of 300,000: 1.5 copies per week.
Sales rank of 500,000: 0.7 copies per week.
Sales rank of 1,000,000: 0.1 copies a week.

(When you see a book with no rank, it means the book has never sold on Amazon).

Here are numbers from another source, showing what sales rank indicates about how long ago a book has sold:

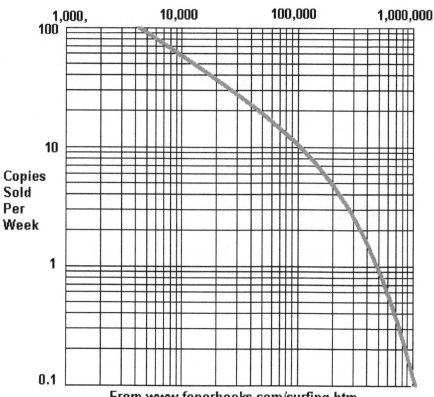

Average Amazon Sales Rank

From www.fonerbooks.com/surfing.htm

1 day	140k
2 days	223k
3 days	427k
4 days	480k
5 days	560k
6 days	629k
1 week	707k
2 weeks	1.17m
3 weeks	1.49m
1 month	1.81m

If this chart is close to accurate (and my experience tells me that it is in the right ballpark), it turns most of what people have assumed about sales rank on its head. By most of what I've read, 1.8 million is considered to be a terrible sales rank, and buying such a book would be an unthinkable crime. But one month isn't that long ago.

When you attempt to reverse-engineer sales rank beyond 2 million, the numbers get too murky to speculate with any accuracy. I can give one powerful example, based on my publishing experience: I published a book on November 15th. It sold a single copy the next day. Then no one else bought it. That book hit a rank of 6 million by January 31st—that's only *2.5 months*. When you consider this, even a rank of 6 million doesn't look that intimidating.

Even if a book is selling only one copy per year, I don't get uncomfortable. I just make sure I'm the next sale, and make sure my margins are huge.

REVERSE ENGINEERING SALES RANK FOR MUSIC AND MOVIES

Amazon has about 30 million books listed, with only about 17 million that have ever sold a copy. That means a book ranked 1 million would be in the top 10% of books sold on Amazon (at that moment). If we can agree that a book ranked 1 million is still very sellable, we can apply this same formula to books and films.

Amazon has listings for:

> 1.2 million movies (VHS and DVD);
> 6 million CDs, cassettes, and vinyl.

Calculating the top 10% of products selling in these categories brings us to these rankings:

> 120,000 in movies;
> 600,000 in music.

The closer you get towards the ranking-threshold, the larger you may want your margins to be before making the investment.

But this is another area where it gets murky, because I know I sell a lot more movies ranked worse than 200,000 (way outside the top 10%) than CDs ranked 200,000 (inside the top 5%). I read this as Amazon simply selling a lot more movies than CDs, which makes a lot of sense. This is an example of how relying on sales rank alone can be deceiving.

Because I sell a lot of movies that aren't ranked within that top 10%, if I think an item has long tail niche appeal, and the price is right, I'll buy it. I recently sold a VHS I bought for 50¢ called Vampire Holocaust. With a title like that, I knew there was a buyer out there that had to have this film. I didn't so much care that the sales rank was 500,000. It sold for $99.99 within two weeks.

EVERYTHING SELLS ON AMAZON, ALMOST: SALES RANK FOR NON-MEDIA

Amazon does not advertise the number of items for sale in each category. Without this figure, you have to way to measure what a "good" sales rank is versus a "bad" rank. Good news: There is a secret hack for this. And I have it for you:

- Select a category from Amazon's home page.
- Enter the following characters into the search field: "[]"
- Hit "go."
- Look at the number of results. That is the total number of products Amazon sells in this category.
- Multiply by .01 (or .05, or .10)

Now we have a number we can use to determine a "good" sales rank in each category. There's no way to know what a rank of 100,000 means if you don't know how many products are in the category.

I did the math so you don't have to, and I'm displayinig in the charts that follow. Amazon is always adding new products to its catalog, so this data will lose its precise accuracy as the years go on. But at the time of this writing it still very useful as a basis for buying decisions.

On the next two pages are the numbers for three formulas: sales rank for the top 10, 5, and 1% in each category. You can choose your comfort level.

Print these and keep them in your wallet as reference. And the next time you're at the outlet store and scan a pack of photo paper with a rank of 12,000, you'll know you're in the safety zone.

Top 10% (Risk-tolerant buying)	Top 5%: (Low-to-mid-range risk)
Books: 1,700,000	Books: 850,000
Movies & TV: 113,117	Movies & TV: 56,559
Music: 511,073	Music: 255,536
Toys & Games: 379,782	Toys & Games: 189,891
Appliances: 48,669	Appliances: 24,335
Arts/Crafts/Sewing: 213,216	Arts/Crafts/Sewing: 106,608
Automotive: 1,244,410	Automotive: 622,205
Baby Products: 76,480	Baby Products: 38,240
Beauty: 167,876	Beauty: 83,938
Cell Phones & Accessories: 4,310,542	Cell Phones & Accessories: 2,155,271
Computers & Accessories: 1,616,710	Computers & Accessories: 808,355
Electronics: 6,358,419	Electronics: 3,179,209
Grocery/Gourmet: 84,781	Grocery/Gourmet: 42,390
Health/Personal Care: 508,006	Health/Personal Care: 254,003
Home & Kitchen: 4,168,840	Home & Kitchen: 2,084,420
Industrial/Scientific: 1,626,360	Industrial/Scientific: 813,180
Musical Instruments: 56,134	Musical Instruments: 28,067
Office Products: 634,600	Office Products: 317,300
Patio/Lawn/Garden: 283,865	Patio/Lawn/Garden: 141,933
Pet Supplies: 89,398	Pet Supplies: 44,699
Software: 40,812	Software: 20,406
Sports & Outdoors: 1,865,427	Sports & Outdoors: 932,714
Tools/Home Improvement: 899,958	Tools/Home Improvement: 449,979
Video Games: 37,320	Video Games: 18,660

A quick note to avoid confusion: These calculations are based on the total number of items for sale in each category (which changes constantly) *except* for books. With books, I based it on the total number of books that have a sales rank (i.e. the items that have sold one ore more copies). Why did I do this? Two reasons: Books are the only category for which I know the approximate number of titles that have a Sales Rank. And two, the book category has one of the lowest percentages of items that have sold a copy (At the time I made this chart, 12 million books have sold while 40 million books are listed). Compare to, say, movies, where 1.14 million DVDs & VHS are listed, and over 1 million have sold. If this doesn't make sense, don't worry. Just defer to the chart and trust I took a lot of time making it accurate.

Top 1%
(Conservative / risk-averse buying)

Books: 170,000
Movies & TV: 11,312
Music: 51,107

Appliances: 4,867
Arts/Crafts/Sewing: 21,322
Automotive: 124,441
Baby Products: 7,648
Beauty: 16,788
Cell Phones & Accessories: 431,054
Computers & Accessories: 161,671
Electronics: 635,842
Grocery/Gourmet: 8,478
Health/Personal Care: 50,801
Home & Kitchen: 416,884
Industrial/Scientific: 162,636
Musical Instruments: 5,613
Office Products: 63,460
Patio/Lawn/Garden: 28,387
Pet Supplies: 8,940
Software: 4,081
Sports & Outdoors: 186,543
Tools/Home Improvement: 89,996
Toys & Games: 37,978

LONG TAIL THEORY: PROFIT WHERE FEW VENTURE

Central to understanding why selling used media on Amazon works, is understanding Long Tail Theory.

The "tail" refers to the long end of the demand curve, as represented on a graph. All the hits fill up the "fat" (short) end of the curve with disproportionate demand, and the vast majority of products that remain occupy the (very long) end of the demand curve – the "long tail."

If you've sold on Amazon for any amount of time, you've heard something along these lines from family or friends: "I have some old books you might want. Real big sellers that people will buy – John Grisham and Steven King!"

This was the old economy—the one where the only money was made at the fat end of the tail, with a few "hits" getting the better part of sales. The non-hits, limited by the shelf space of retailers with finite square footage, were doomed to obscurity and unprofitability.

And then came the Internet.

And then came Amazon – "The largest store in the world."

Constraints of physical space were obliterated. Limitations of distribution were eradicated. Disparities of access vanished. With the Internet, a copy of *The Principles of Helicopter Aerodynamics* is just as accessible as *The Hunger Games*. An online retailer is just as likely to give "shelf space" to *Voodoo Rituals of New Guinea Pygmy Tribes* as *Treasure Island*, because there is no shelf space—just pixels. And consumer's purchases aren't limited by what retailers put in front of them in a store—they have equal access to nearly every book ever printed.

The old rules are dead.

Here are the key components of the Long Tail Theory, in short:

- The Internet drives demand away from hit products with mass appeal and directs that demand to more obscure niche items.

- As the Internet makes distribution easier, demand shifts from the most popular products at the head of a demand curve to the long tail made up of demand for many different niche products.

- As purchasing paths shift from retail shelf space and geography to keyword searches, customers will increasingly be lead down the long tail towards niche products.

A few quotes from Chris Anderson, the originator of this theory (from his site www.LongTail.com):

" The theory of the Long Tail is that our culture and economy is increasingly shifting away from a focus on a relatively small number of "hits" (mainstream products and markets) at the head of the demand curve and toward a huge number of niches in the tail."

" As the costs of production and distribution fall, especially online, there is now less need to lump products and consumers into one-size-fits-all containers. In an era without the constraints of physical shelf space and other bottlenecks of distribution, narrowly-target goods and services can be as economically attractive as mainstream fare."

" Traditional retail economics dictate that stores only stock the likely hits, because shelf space is expensive. But online retailers (from

Amazon to iTunes) can stock virtually everything, and the number of available niche products outnumber the hits by several orders of magnitude. Those millions of niches are the Long Tail, which had been largely neglected until recently in favor of the Short Head of hits."

Everything on Amazon is available equally to everything else. There are no end-cap displays. There are no "featured titles" (not really). There is only a search bar, where everyone with an obscure interest finds their book. If you like exploring storm drains, you'll find *Access All Areas: A User's Guide to the Art of Urban Exploration*. If you like being a cat burglar, you'll find *Confessions of a Master Jewel Thief*.

Boundaries of distribution and inventory-on-hand have been erased. If you're into something weird, three clicks and the book is at your house tomorrow.

People don't have an interest in "traveling" or "golf." Nor do they buy books on "traveling" or "golf." Their true interests, when they are allowed to express them through limitless purchasing options, are more refined. They are interested in getting jobs on stranger's yachts and seeing the world for free, or yoga routines that will improve their golf game. With the Internet making products catered to these narrow interests more accessible, people's attention—and purchases—will also drift in more refined directions.

In short: The economy and culture is shifting from mass markets to millions of niches. Homogenized chain stores don't define our purchases any longer. We can find and buy almost anything we choose.

What does this mean for Amazon sellers?

It means when I'm sourcing I go for the books on underground alien bases before I go for Dilbert comic strip collections. It's counterintuitive but important to understand: the more obscure, the more likely it is to be profitable on Amazon.

It also means that when your mom offered you her Grisham novels, she had it all wrong. In the Internet economy, the money for lone-wolf booksellers is not in the mass-market hits. It's in the long tail.

THE LONG TAIL TEST

I created The Long Tail Test as a solution for one common dilemma: how to separate a valuable-but-poorly-ranked book you shouldn't buy, from a valuable-but-poorly-ranked book you *should*.

It happens all the time: You find a copy of *Psychiatric Care of Organ Transplant Patients*. Lowest price: $75. Sales rank: 3,200,000. How do you determine if this book will find an eventual buyer, or if it is merely obsolete?

Give it the Long Tail Test.

There are books that have a very small demand, but a demand nonetheless; and there are books that are likely to never sell another copy again for the rest of time—they have been completely forgotten.

You need to know the difference. You do that by asking these questions:

The test

- Is it on a subject so esoteric or niche that there are unlikely to be any other books ever printed on this exact subject? (Use your best judgment.)

- Is the book on a subject that has not been made obsolete by time? (As opposed to a copy of *Repairing Your PC* from 1984)

- Is it published for a specialized, niche audience? (As opposed to a broader, mainstream audience. For example: *The CIA Manual for Surveillance in Jungle Environments* vs. *Yacht Maintenance for Dummies*.)

- Is it non-fiction?

- Is it published by a legitimate publishing house (i.e. *not* self-published)?

- Is it the only edition published (i.e. *not* one of several updated editions printed)?

- Is it *not* a textbook, which will usually have multiple editions? (sorry for the stilted phrasing here.)

- Is the book offering value to the reader that is not likely to have been improved upon in other books since its publication? (Again, use your best judgment.)

If the answer is "yes" to every question, buy it. It will find a buyer eventually.

If you're still on the fence, ask this one:

- Is it *weird?* Does it make you say: *Someone wrote a book about this?!*

If a book passes the test, I don't care what its rank is. I don't mind sitting on a book for two years if I paid 50¢ for it and it's going to make me $50.

What is important is a huge margin. Because when you're buying books ranked 2 million or 3 million and up, you have to approach it with the expectation that some of the books will never sell. If I have 100 long tail books that cost me $100 total but the margins are huge, I only need to sell two or three of those books to break even. And when any of the next 97 sell, it's all profit.

The question to never ask is: *Who would want this?!* The answer only has to be: *Someone... eventually.*

THE LONG TAIL OF OFFICE PRODUCTS?

You can apply your own version of the Long Tail Test to non-book categories. But this is where it starts to get a little weird, so proceed with caution. Pet Supplies is a much more volatile category than Books. There is very little a discontinued brand of cat litter has to offer that isn't exceeded by those you can find at Pet Smart, and you're probably better off leaving that bag ranked 200,000 right there on the shelf at Overstock Depot.

A Long Tail Test for non-media might look like this:

Is the item still relevant (versus obsolete)?

Is it likely to have collector value?

Does it satisfy a need that cannot be met by a newer or less expensive product?

Is it a discontinued item people are likely to have a loyalty to?

Is it a discontinued item that functions as an accessory for something likely to still be in use?

…and so on.

There is a longer long tail in Toys than, for example, in Health & Beauty. This is simply because there is a greater percentage of products in Toys that will sell "now and then"—items with niche appeal that will be sought out by the right buyer (like a collector) every so often.

Success will depend on a mix of asking the right questions and a honed intuition. But because margins tend to be smaller outside of media categories, I like to stay within the top 5%.

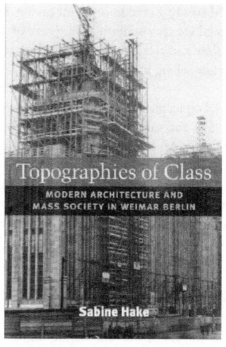

No.   Yes.

MY EVOLUTION OF BUYING LOW AND SELLING HIGH – PART II

With the FBA "silent sales machine" rumbling onward, making me money whether I got out of bed or not, I began to feed the machine with increasingly longer long tail items: books ranked worse than 1 million; then 1.5 million; then 2 million and up.

If I found a book (or DVD, or VHS, or anything) that passed the Long Tail Test, and the margins were big, I bought it. The worse the rank, the larger the margins I needed to see if I was going to add it to my inventory. But I began consistently buying items of a rank that everything I'd read told me never to touch.

The first several months of this approach did not instill much confidence. You sell a book here and there, but when you're looking at several hundred dollars invested in a book stratum that is only bringing the occasional sale, all the math is telling you to change course and start doing damage control by getting those books out of your inventory.

As my long tail inventory increased, sales started to become more frequent and steady. I could not count on any one book selling anytime soon, but I could always count on selling *some* of them soon. In aggregate, they produced a slow and steady revenue stream that operated by different laws than my better-selling inventory.

As a concept, it's almost stupidly simple: buy a high volume of poor-selling books, and sales will trickle in, slow but steady. The more you buy, the more that sell. And the huge margins guarantee that you're never losing money.

Through developing a comfort in delayed return, I have produced a steady addition to my FBA income. I estimate I make an additional $800 per month off these long tail books. As I add to this layer of my inventory, I expect in very short time to be making an extra $1,500 per month off these books that "will never sell."

Should I be concerned about a glut of long-tail books entering the Amazon marketplace after publishing this? Probably not. Most people encouraged by this will simply buy the wrong books. At the end of the day, the Long Tail Test is still largely subjective. To use it correctly requires a primarily intuitive understanding of books that I don't think most people will ever have. I have proven my ability to separate long tail books that will sell from long tail books that will languish. Most simply won't ever develop that subconscious process that separates the books with extreme niche appeal from those that simply have no audience.

As of this writing, I probably have 1000 titles in my inventory ranked worse than 1.5 million. These are books nearly all the gurus will tell you to avoid. They were purchased for anywhere from one cent to $20 with no promise (or hope) of them selling anytime soon. Each one passed my Long Tail Test and that's all I need.

The guiding consideration in most buying purchases is: How quickly do you need your investment back?

The risk-averse strategy I began with is a legitimate way to start. And as your discretionary income grows, so should your tolerance for risk. With more money, you should get comfortable having some of it tied up for longer periods in obscure books and media that may not sell tomorrow—or even anytime this year.

Today I earn enough via FBA to take moderate risks, and most of them pay off—eventually. I can walk up to a church rummage sale while people are elbowing each other to get a slice, and offer the organizer $200 for every book if he'll put a blanket over the table while I back up my truck. I'll buy huge collections of conspiracy theory books for hundreds of dollars sight unseen, just because I know that genre holds its value and I'm willing to take the risk. Life serves the risk-taker.0

HOW TO INTERPRET FBA APP DATA

Scan an item, any item. Then show the results to five people and you will get five different interpretations of the data. Some will say "buy, buy, buy." Some will say "pass, pass, pass." Some will say "It depends…" Few people know how to interpret the data effectively.

You should have a set profit threshold you need to see before making a purchase. All other factors being in your favor, this bottom-line number will tell you if you should buy or pass. I always aim for making three times my investment (getting $3 back for every $1 I invest).

If you could track my eye movements when the FBA Scan results show up on my screen, it might go in this order:

1. Merchant-fulfilled price
First stop is the lowest MF offer. This will be used as a baseline to determine the competitiveness of the lowest FBA offer.

2. FBA offers
I then see if the lowest FBA offer is reasonable, relative to the lowest MF offer. I will click through to Amazon to view this data if the app won't display it (it usually won't).

3. Net payout
Knowing my cost, I check the net payout. I'm aiming for three times my investment, unless I know it will turn over very fast, in which case I am comfortable getting 2x.

4. Sales rank/department
These two are inseparable because the relevance of a sales rank number is relative to the number of total items for sale in a category.

I have already jumped ahead a little, because net payout is irrelevant if the sales rank is outside my comfort zone. I usually want rank to be at least in the top 25%, but I am much more comfortable in the top 5%. I refer to the sales rank breakdown I keep in my wallet for categories I'm less familiar with to know what rank gets me in the top 5% or 25%.

5. Amazon's price
I will then double-check to make sure existing FBA offers are not more than Amazon's price. (Amazon changes its prices often, and it regularly happens that the price drops below all existing FBA offers.)

6. Back to FBA offers
If the item is well-ranked, I will revisit FBA offers and omit the lowest FBA offer as competition. Instead, I will focus on the second and third as the only items I'm competing against (this is assuming the lowest offer only has one unit for sale). If the item is very *very* well ranked, I will look at the 3th or possibly even the 4th offer.

If everything checks out, it will be in a box and off to Amazon the next day.

MARGIN SELLER VS. VOLUME SELLER

This is where you make a decision: Are you a margin seller or a volume seller? The margin seller takes anything with the right margin-to-rank ratio. She'll go home with a poor-selling item that may take months or years to sell, *if* the payoff is big enough.

The volume seller buys well-ranked items and a lot of them, even if the margins are small. These are the sellers pricing books at $3.99, taking home maybe 50 cents per book after costs, hoping to "make up for it in volume."

My approach: Be both.

As I explained in the Long Tail section, I deal in poorly-ranked items if the margins are big.

I also deal in small-margin items if I know they will turn over quickly. With books, this means I will sell a book for $7.50 and take home $3 if it's ranked 1,000 and is virtually guaranteed to sell same-day.

Choose your own path. And when you do, know the numbers. That's what this chapter is for.

FBA PRICING STRATEGY: INTELLIGENT PRICING FOR MAXIMUM PROFITS

5

PRICING FOR THE FBA ENVIRONMENT
THE #1 RULE OF FBA
MY PRICING STRATEGY
TEXTBOOK GOLD
MOTHER OF ALL FBA SALES

FBA PRICING STRATEGY: GETTING THE LAST LAUGH THROUGH SUPERIOR PRICING

Pricing is unquestionably the most misunderstood and fumbled part of FBA. Everything comes down to how intelligently you set your price. Too low, and there's money left on the table. Too high, and you'll be sitting on an item that isn't selling.

The good news is that with a well-ranked item on FBA, there almost is no "too high."

The primary culprit in bad pricing is people transitioning from "the old way of doing things" to FBA, but not radically changing their pricing strategy. A solid pricing formula has to be in harmony with the FBA environment.

In simple terms: People price things too low. It costs them money, and forces the rest of us to play their bottom-feeding game or hold out until they've sold out.

I like the gem of business wisdom that goes: If it sells right away, you priced it too low.

Conversely, if it doesn't sell right away, it does not mean you've priced too high — it just means you've priced too high for that day. Or week. There will be a time in the near future when the price you set is the right price, and you'll get the sale.

I have a pricing strategy that I believe is a good one based on my experience. It has brought me consistent top-dollar for my inventory. Clearly, it is not a strategy adhered to by some other FBA sellers, but it is one that has provided steady profit to me over my 12 months using FBA.

These principles should guide your strategy. Repeat them to yourself as though mantras:

> You are competing for Amazon Prime subscribers and those wanting free Super Saver Shipping — *no one else.*

> Buyers are willing to pay much more for your items because you're offering what others can't: free second-day shipping, a no-questions-asked

72

return policy, super-fast standard shipping, free tracking, and the built-in trust Amazon has obtained with customers over nearly 20 years. Every one of these adds value to your item that makes it far more appealing than the same merchant fulfilled item.

You **do not** have to be the next sale. You do not **want** to be the next sale. You want to be the highest-priced sale the market can bear – whether in a week or six months.

RECIPE FOR DISASTER: THE SHORTEST DISTANCE BETWEEN YOU AND AN UNPROFITABLE FBA

Currently, some of the dumbest human beings on this planet or any other are FBA sellers.

Here are a few of their names:

Jenson_books_inc
Apex_media
New Chapter Recycling
Textbooksrus FBA

Why do I call them out by name? Because the owners aren't in arm's reach for me to backhand. Maybe seeing their names in lights will finally sober them to sanity, but I doubt it.

Simply put, they price their books like morons, force prices down, and totally don't get FBA. These people have *no idea* what they are doing and should be shamed out of walking the streets freely. Being big doesn't mean you're not a total moron about running a business.

Their crime is a complete failure to understand the business they are in and their customers, the FBA buyer. They would more quickly achieve their goals by just sitting back in their warehouses and burning piles of money with flamethrowers.

THE FIRST AND ONLY COMMANDMENT

If FBA was a religion, it would only have one Commandment:

Thou shalt not underprice any FBA seller.

Thou shalt not underprice any FBA seller.

Thou shalt not underprice any FBA seller.

Thou shalt not underprice any FBA seller.

Thou shalt not underprice any FBA seller

THOU SHALT NOT UNDER-PRICE ANY FBA SELLER.

Anyone who violates this commandment undermines the benefits of FBA. You may get your 60¢ from that $4 sale, but you only hurt yourself.

At the bottom of the tablet, there is some fine print to the Commandment. I won't hesitate to underprice an FBA seller if their price is in fundamental conflict with my pricing strategy.

This is where it gets somewhat subjective, but here are some examples of where I feel it is acceptable to underprice other FBA sellers:

- An item that is poorly ranked (e.g. with books, worse than 1 million), and the lowest FBA price is more than $3.99 above the lowest non-FBA price. These are the long tail items that should be priced to sell, because sales are low enough that Amazon Prime customers may only come around once a year - or less.

- An item with an FBA price that is set unrealistically high. Again, there is a subjective formula at work, but I would apply "unrealistic" to items with a MF price of under $25, and the lowest FBA price more than $15 above that. (This excludes textbooks. I will price very high with decently-ranked textbooks and usually get the sale eventually). Remember that sales rank is the overriding factor here. I won't weigh you down with the details of my personal algorithm, but it is a calculation based on price and type of book with sales rank as the pivot point.

- The lowest FBA seller has an item priced more than Amazon's offer. Amazon is always the ceiling.

Do not participate in the suicidal "race to the bottom." Although it is to some extent an inevitability in any market, it is a travesty seeing a forced acceleration in this direction by sloppy businesspeople. I see sellers setting their repricers to underprice their competition by 5 cents several times a day, or just desperately chasing conversion as though it was a religion. I've watched the price on high-demand items go through the floor because of short-sighted sellers desperate to be the next sale.

It's not worth it.

HERE IS THE NEW FBA MANTRA

The shortest way to ensure FBA becomes unprofitable for everyone and its potential is squandered by amateurs chasing nickels is *to be the lowest price*.

Again for effect: The biggest mistake you can make as an FBA seller is to price an item at or below the lowest priced offer.

The second biggest mistake: Setting the price on a fast-selling, well-ranked book only $3.99 above the lowest non-FBA offer. In a desperate move to grab the top spot, many (most?) FBA sellers will leave money on the table by pricing only $3.99 above the lowest MF offer. This gives them the top spot and the quickest sale, but I'm pretty sure the measure of a business is its profits—not the turnover of its inventory.

FBA sellers are adding way more than $3.99 in value. Free second day shipping, free tracking, hassle-free returns… We are the VIP section of the world's biggest store, pricing ourselves for the clearance aisle.

The practice of underpricing items is so pervasive, the only sense I can make of this is that FBA is being taken over by heroin addicts. People in such a desperate need to get their next fix that they will throw money out the window for the sake of getting the next sale. Only junkies behave like this.

This mistake of pricing only $3.99 higher is even encouraged by some within the FBA seller community. For books of a certain (medium-to-poor) sales rank, this is a smart strategy. But across the board? Lunacy.

But a lot of people do it. Why? Several reasons:

1. They're lazy. It's a very easy formula to just match the lowest price (or go a flat $3.99 above) and move on to the next listing.
2. Failure to understand the business they're in and the psychology of FBA customers.
3. Stubbornness. Stuck in the old (merchant-fulfilled) model, they are unable or unwilling to adapt.
4. Disbelief. They understand *why* others price higher, but don't believe it works.
5. The cult of "volume". Some sellers with tens or hundreds of thou-

sands of items in their inventory are so focused on getting it out the door, they fail to see they would sell their items nearly as quickly by charging 50% to 300% more.

THE BOTTOM-FEEDERS: WHY PEOPLE SELL BOOKS FOR 3.99 (AND LESS)

Cutthroat competition has lead to a downward spiral of prices, with desperate sellers underpricing each other, leading to many sellers even selling books at a loss.

Why does this happen?

First, the absolute lowest price a merchant-fulfilled seller can charge for a book is one penny. If you're selling an average-sized book, you come away with a profit of about 12¢ per book (after postage credit and fees).

In theory, an FBA seller shouldn't have a reason to price lower than $4. That price gives them the top spot, above all the one-cent sellers. That is until the next FBA seller prices their copy at $3.99. Then the race to the bottom gets uglier.

Right now, a seller selling an average-sized book breaks even (nets absolutely nothing) at around $3.50. Yet you will see a **ton** of books listed for less. What's going on here?

There are a few theories, from repricers gone wild to mega-sellers who just don't know the numbers. What's interesting to me is that no one knows. I have never seen any mega-seller actually speak up and explain themselves.

Just don't play their game and try to compete: It's a loser's game played by bottom-feeders. Ignore media items with crowded competition in the $3.99 to $5.99 range. Keep your margins high and your dignity intact.

LEADING BY EXAMPLE: MY PERSONAL PRICING STRATEGY

There's a lot of talk about how no single approach to selling on Amazon works for everyone. For example, some people are addicted to heroin and need money now.

Keeping in mind Amazon's price is always the ceiling, I'll lay out my pricing strategy for books:

Ranked better than 5,000: I'll price $15 above the lowest merchant-fulfilled (MF) price—or more. The exact amount depends on my assessment of the perceived value of the book (whether it is a small-sized novel or a large scholarly tome). For books like these that are selling 10+ copies a day, there is someone in the near future who will assign $15 in value to second day shipping. (Remember, $12 is Amazon's default charge for second-day shipping, and not all sellers offer this option.) In the case of textbooks, I will go $30 to $50 above if there is no FBA competition.

5,000—10,000: If the gap is more than 50 cents, I'll position myself as the second-lowest FBA offer. If there are no FBA offers, I will price $12 to $15 more. (Again, this is always excluding textbooks—FBA offers seem to sell at nearly any price.)

10,000—100,000: I'll position myself as the lowest FBA price. If I get significantly under-priced, by one or two offers, I won't be afraid to hold my original price. Books that hold this rank are doing enough volume that my offer will sell eventually. If no other FBA offers, I will price $10 or $12 above the lowest non-FBA price.

100,000—600,000: I'll price $6 to $10 above the lowest non-FBA price, depending on the cover price. Where there are other competing FBA offers, I'll position myself as the second-lowest if the lowest is less than $3.99 above the lowest MF offer. If it's above, I will match.

600,000—1 million: This is the range in which I start to keep my price a flat $3.99 above the lowest MF price, and match any FBA price if it's under the $3.99 threshold. With textbooks, if it's not in the middle of textbook season (August/Sept & January), I will price penny books at $14.99, with the hope that demand will surge next time the school bell rings.

1 million and up: I'll price a flat $3.99 above. You don't know how far or fast these titles will slip down the sales rank, and I aim to be the next sale. This is the range in which you *are* chasing the next sale, because you don't know when—or if—it will come.

Again: Textbooks are an exception, always. There seems to be no limit as to how much more people will pay for an FBA textbook. I will price any textbook ranked better than 1 million at $10 above the lowest merchant fulfilled offer. Better than 500,000, I'll go $15 to $25. Better than 100,000, I'll go $20 to $40.

A note about evolutionary economics: Humans are wired to think of increases in price in terms of percentages, not hard numbers. For example, a buyer is much more likely to spend $125 for an FBA offer where the lowest non-FBA offer is $100 than they are to spend $35 where the lowest non-FBA offer is $10. That extra $25 is processed differently. Keep this fact in mind when pricing.

A word on the $35 free shipping mark: If I am pricing between $30 and $35, and I won't be going over Amazon's price, I'll often raise the price to a flat $35. This is the point at which everyone's order qualifies for free shipping. Remember the stats: 38% of my customers over a 30-day period were non-Prime subscribers who bought (presumably) because of the free shipping option. Even if they're paying a little more, everyone likes "free", and many will just go straight for the item that offers free shipping.

With CDs, videos, and non-media, you scale accordingly. Use your intuition, and pay attention to how much higher than non-FBA offers you can get away with pricing items in various categories. Determine at what price point they sell quickly, and what causes them to languish.

FAST NICKEL VS. SLOW DIME

When I price, I price high and hold my ground, taking the slow $9.99 sale over the quick $5.99 sale. My turnaround is slower, but my per-item profit is far above the average seller's. (Over the last 60 days, my average sales price was $15.33.) I don't have any current drug or spending addictions, and don't need to concern myself with sacrificing profit for the quick reward. I'll take delayed gratification that brings greater profit (and dignity) than a desperate pursuit of the next sale.

There is an abundance mindset at work that you might do well to cultivate in yourself. One where no single inventory item takes on any significance. You no longer think of your inventory as a collection of individual parts that each must be maintained. Your inventory is a symphony of profit, a beating organism that pumps money into you bank account in a steady rhythm—not a barreling tidal wave.

Some will misread this as advocating lazy, sloppy business: ignoring poor performing, profit-draining problem spots and letting weeds grow in the garden in favor of a Pollyanna fantasy where "it will all sell one day."

To preemptively address that, I will say this: By all means, do regular diagnostic checks on your inventory. Run a repricer (with carefully managed criteria) *sometimes*. Purge poorly-ranked items whose prices have fallen below profitability. Do these things. But don't do them often.

Focus on the quality and volume of your inventory, and the quality and volume of your sales will follow.

It's the difference between the diversified, buy-and-hold stock investor and the day trader. Everyone makes money in the stock market with a diversified portfolio over a ten-year period. Other people sit before a panopticon of monitors, watching numbers whirl by in a Herculean exercise of micromanagement. I get both models. I just don't think the latter is intelligent business with FBA.

No single item matters. It's all numbers: When you have thousands of items in inventory, and all of them are priced 25% or 100% or more above the lowest seller, you are still selling steadily, making money, and enjoying profit margins far beyond your competition—your short-sighted, nickel-chasing competition.

The others are going to sell out, and you'll be next in line for the sale. You'll be offering a pricier option, but price is not the sole factor in buying decisions, especially to Amazon Prime subscribers. You're offering what merchant-fulfilled sellers aren't. Your customers are willing to pay more for this, and they will. If you let them.

Adopt the mindset that if any item isn't selling, it doesn't matter. What matters is that many of them are selling. And steadily. And when they do, you're making 5 or 10 or 50 times what you paid for them, and 2 or 3 times what the last seller did. Someone else may beat you to the next sale, but with a selling price double theirs, you'll get the last laugh.

FBA GOLD WITH TEXTBOOKS

Textbooks are one category in which you can price far, *far* above competing non-FBA offers and still get the sale. This is a huge category with big profits for those who price intelligently.

Sometime around the second week in August, and the first week of January, you'll hear a faint tremor in the distance... Shortly, your account will blow up with sales from students all over the country buying your textbooks. And not just books that are overtly "textbooks"—anything that gets used in a classroom sees a surge in sales.

Textbooks are the perfect recipe for FBA:

Urgency. Textbook purchases are usually time-sensitive, and delivery is needed on short notice by a fixed date. This is where free second-day shipping is a major selling point.

Amazon Student program. The Amazon Student program offers six months of Amazon Prime for free, making students a disproportionately large percentage of Prime subscribers (Amazon doesn't release exact figures).

To illustrate, last week I sold a textbook for *$45 more* than the lowest non-FBA price in the same condition. Many students just won't bet their grade on the potential for a slow merchant-fulfilled purchase arriving on an unknown date.

And just prior to each textbook season, I will go through and reprice every well-ranked textbook manually to a *slightly* unreasonable price, knowing there is a better-than-not chance during these periods that it will find a buyer.

Not staying on top of textbook prices during this time can be costly. I recently noticed the price of a textbook I sold for $60 had jumped to $150. Someone got a deal-and-a-half because I failed to catch it and reprice upwards.

CASE CLOSED

Just as final edits were being made on this book, something happened that was almost as though the universe was conspiring to oversell my point. I made a sale that shocked even me.

I sold a book for $104 more than the lowest non-FBA offer.

Same condition. *One hundred and four dollars.*

The book was consistently ranked in the top 5,000, and in the weeks after purchasing it, other sellers had run the price down from $100 to $16. As the only FBA seller, I held my $130 price and of course *still got the sale.*

These are the prices Prime subscribers are willing to pay. *If you let them.*

BOOK GRADING: NOT WHAT YOU THINK

6

HEDGING YOUR BETS
WHAT IS NEW CONDITION?
GRADING USED BOOKS

WHITE LIES AND HEDGED BETS: HOW TO GRADE BOOKS FOR AMAZON

There is a lot of confusion over what each book condition category means. Ultimately, Amazon's definitions are much less relevant than how they are interpreted by customers.

When listing a book, you are given the options of New, Like New, Very Good, Good, Acceptable, and Collectible.

Here is Amazon's official word on each:

> "*New*: Just like it sounds. A brand-new, unused, unread copy in perfect condition."

> "*Like New*: An apparently unread copy in perfect condition. Dust cover is intact, with no nicks or tears. Spine has no signs of creasing. Pages are clean and are not marred by notes or folds of any kind. Book may contain a remainder mark on an outside edge but this should be noted in listing comments."

> "*Very Good*: A copy that has been read, but remains in excellent condition. Pages are intact and are not marred by notes or highlighting. The spine remains undamaged."

> "*Good*: A copy that has been read, but remains in clean condition. All pages are intact, and the cover is intact (including dust cover, if applicable). The spine may show signs of wear. Pages can include limited notes and highlighting, and the copy can include "From the library of" labels."

> "*Acceptable*: A readable copy. All pages are intact, and the cover is intact (the dust cover may be missing). Pages can include considerable notes--in pen or highlighter--but the notes cannot obscure the text."

Your goal is to satisfy the customer. Or if you're a glass-half-empty person, to *not* get negative feedback.

I've found that negative feedback arises from customers disputing your choice of a *used* category (LN, VG, G, or A) much more often than people ordering a new book and arguing it is not new.

For this reason, and the often huge price difference between used and new books, I'm going to give special attention to our first question:

WHAT IS NEW CONDITON?

I used to spend a lot of time holding used books up to the light at thrift stores, wondering if I could list them as new. I disqualified anything with a bumped corner, or slight fray to the dustjacket. If it wasn't bookstore-new, I wasn't going to chance the negative feedback.

One day I ordered a book from myself to give as a gift. The book was among the most "new"- new books I had, purchased right off the discount book table at Barnes & Noble.

What arrived two days later was a very imperfect book. The edges of the dustjacket had wear along the top. The new book sheen was gone. And every corner had some perceptible level of trauma. It was worse than thousands of books I had dismissed as used at thrift stores and book sales, and subsequently passed on.

This was a major lightbulb moment. My customers were never receiving "new" books.

Amazon has shipped out thousands of my books as new that have arrived with a similar level of wear, and I have *never* received negative feedback for this.

My books were being tossed into trucks, thrown onto conveyor belts, shelved, and then pulled, packaged, and thrown onto another truck—all before reaching the customer.

This is what I learned: Buyers understand a book sent through the mail will have a level of wear they would not expect from a new book bought off the shelf.

It became apparent that buyers don't buy books in "new" condition because they want a cosmetically flawless book. They buy for other reasons. Among them:

> The psychological satisfaction of having bought a "new" book. Similar to buying tap water in a bottle versus drinking right out of the tap, or spending $10,000 more on a new car versus a flawless used car with only

a few thousand miles.

The guaranteed absence of marks, highlighting, writing, etc. This holds especially true for buyers of new textbooks.

The "why not?" factor with books whose used price is close to that of a new copy.

I can't say I understand the motives of the new-condition book buyer, often paying two to fifteen times (or beyond) more than they would for a used counterpart. Some of those are gifts, but there are a lot of people whose motives are, let's just say... materialistic.

To be clear: I am not advising selling damaged, worn books as "New." I am advising selling new books *that have had a previous owner, and may or may not have been gently read* as New. If it is cosmetically flawless, it's "New." That's it.

The time *not* to cut corners is on highly collectible books. When the seller is paying $30, $50, or $200 more for new condition—that's what you should deliver. This is best achieved by not only shipping in a genuinely new book, but shipping it to Amazon protected with bubble wrap (see "Shipping").

I don't really care what Amazon thinks of this, but today easily less than 10% of the books I sell as "new" are in fact unread copies. Every seller does it: You find a new-looking book, shine the cover up at home, and ship it to Amazon as "new." It could have even been read by its previous owner, but most sellers know that "new" means "cosmetically flawless," not "having no previous owner."

All the matters with grading is giving the customer what they expect. If you deliver it (in this case, a flawless book), whether or not it had a previous owner is an insignificant, academic detail.

In a later chapter, I go into the importance of maintaining a good feedback rating on Amazon. When selling with FBA, all other variables are handled by Amazon, and the only factor in your control that affects feedback is proper grading.

GRADING "LESS THAN NEW" BOOKS

Through the inspiration of some negative feedback (none of it received for

the aforementioned grading strategy for previously-owned "new" books) that
almost had me kicked off Amazon, I learned this grading strategy:

Grade "nearly new" books as New.
Grade like-new books as Very Good.
Grade only very *very* good books as Very Good.
Grade merely very good books as Good.
Grade good books as Good.
Grade acceptable books as Acceptable, and be *very* detailed about the damage.

SOURCING CHECKLIST: GOING WHERE THE MONEY IS

7

THE LIST

BIG SOURCIN'

On my desk I keep a binder with fifteen pages listing every inventory source in a 90-minute radius; with addresses, hours, and notes. As of today, it comes to 64 sources for books and media. I visit each an average of once per month. I go out four weekdays per week, averaging less than four hours per trip on three of those. In addition, I do the rummage and yard sale circuit until noon on Saturdays. (My list doesn't include non-fixed inconsistent sources, such as Craigslist and the occasional auction.)

(A brief disclaimer here: I've lived in many parts of the country, and my current location is probably the thrift store capital of the planet. I have never lived anywhere that has close to as many sources).

Over the last two months, my Amazon payments have averaged $7,000 per month.

The next piece of math was hard to do, but I calculated my profit from wholesale or non-fixed sources was $1,000 per month (margin of error +/- $200).

This leaves $6,000 per month from the fixed locations in my binder.

What this comes to is just under $100 profit per source—a very reasonable number. It's totally realistic to expect $100 profit per month from any decent source—whether a thrift store or library bookstore. A lot of these average me only $20 per month, while a couple consistently bring me $1,000.

Over this same two-month period, my average sales price per item was $15.33. This translates to an average payout of $10.21.

At $100 per source and $10.21 per book, I only need to extract an average of ten items from every source. Again, very reasonable. Some will offer hundreds of items a month. Many will only have four or five. But to maintain a $6,000 per month average, I only need to get my hands on *ten items per source.*

The point of this is one very important lesson: Your profit is in direct proportion to the number of your sources. If you know you can safely average $100 per source, you can do the math on exactly how many sources you need to reach your desired income. If you desire nothing more than $1,000 per month, your mission right now is to find ten consistent sources of inventory.

Want $2,000? Find twenty.

There are factors outside your control—such as your competition and the quality of your source's inventory. Ignore those. Focus on what you can control: locating sources. And then locating more.

Let's focus on getting you to those first ten sources. Note that there are other, even better FBA models outside the scope of this book. For instance, the sellers who source from a single wholesaler and bring in $30,000 per month. Because our focus here is used media, I am providing this chapter as a guide to get you to those first ten sources.

BOOK SOURCING: THE CHECKLIST

What follows is a starter list of the most common used-media sources. Following this, I give a more thorough look at personal sources I use which either have not read mentioned in other FBA guides, are underrepresented, or underrated.

Yard Sales
A fruitful staple. Check *Craigslist.com* or *YardSaleSearch.com* and filter by searching "books". Generally, people just want items at their yard sales gone, especially the books, and you can get amazing deals by asking: *How much for all of them?"*

Thrift Stores
These are your cash cow. Search Google Maps for "thrift store" or visit *TheThriftShopper.com* (only lists non-profit stores). Hit them often and hit them hard.

Library Book Sales
Most libraries will have a book sale at least once a year. Some of them are truly massive. Unfortunately the larger the sale, the more ruthless the

Rummage Sales

In advance of a large rummage sale, call the group organizing (usually a church or school) and ask if you can view the donations in advance of the sale. I emphasize that I am interested in buying in volume, and will pay 50% more than the standard price (which is usually 25¢ to $1) per book. If they hesitate, I offer to spend at least $50 or pay 100% more. I also emphasize that I am generally interested in books for a specialty market, and will be leaving most popular titles (which Amazon is already saturated with) for the day-of-sale customers.

Thrift Stores

These are your bread and butter, so let me give a couple notes on thrift stores...

I've worked at thrift stores, and I can tell you that if a thrift store isn't putting out large volumes of books consistently, they are probably going into the trash. One thrift store I worked at in high school was in an affluent suburb. As a sorter, I was consistently told to throw away boxes of items directly off the back of someone's truck — often times books. Books are not seen as profit centers for thrift stores, and because of the weight, volume, and low price, they can be seen as more burdensome than profitable.

While working at this thrift store, we were forbidden from taking home items that were slated for the dumpster. Even as a teenager, it was simple to spot a potentially collectible book, and I consistently smuggled out throwaways for resale to local bookstores. A couple of titles I still remember are a leather-bound collection of Lord Byron poetry from the 1700s, and an original copy of *Prairie Fire*, the manifesto of the 1970s US guerrilla group the Weather Underground. These rare titles were slated to be thrown away by ignorant thrift store managers that looked at books as heavy, cumbersome, and unprofitable.

Although this would work at any thrift store, I like to note thrift stores that appear either to not put out many books, or to clearly have more books than space for them. I find the manager and ask if they ever have more books than they want, or otherwise would be interested in selling in bulk. I've arranged many large pickups of several thousand books from stores this way.

competition. The sales with the most potential are those that are **not** listed on *BookSaleFinder.com*. Anything listed on this site attracts sellers within a three-hour radius, making your job difficult. A lot of sellers are abandoning these to the weekend warrior sellers, while others still consider library sales to be their bread and butter.

Estate Sales
Best potential for high-end and collectible books. Also best potential for

exorbitant prices.

Auctions

Auctions take many forms, from thrift store castaway auctions to company liquidations. At a general auction, books are close to the bottom of things anyone is going to bid on. You have a good chance of coming away with a pallet of books for one dollar. See the "University Surplus Stores & Auctions" section for more.

Local Classifieds

These are waning in use in the age of Craigslist. The good news is that anyone selling large lots of books via printed classified ads is totally internet-ignorant and hasn't looked up the value of their books on Amazon. Worth a look.

Garage Sales

In the past eight days, I've filled my truck twice by asking a garage sale host: "Do you have any more books in the house you'd like to sell?" Earlier today, a woman invited me into her home and sold me her entire collection of art, photography, marketing, and martial arts books. I offered her $10 for every 50-gallon tub I could fill. The total came to $60. As I type this in a Starbucks, I haven't even been home to do the numbers, but I'm expecting to clear at least $1000 off this purchase.

Flea Markets

People with hundreds or thousands of books to unload often set up shop at a flea market or swap meet. Last weekend I found an Amazon seller selling his leftovers. He clearly wasn't using FBA, because I came away with boxes of books at 50¢ a title.

Publisher Remainder Sales

Keep all eyes open for remainder sales by niche publishers, university presses, etc.

Library Bookstores

A lot of libraries have bookstores built-in, run by Friends of the Library. People whose local libraries don't have bookstores have a hard time believing these exist, but they are very common. It takes me three four-hour work days to get through my local library bookstore. It's obscene how much money they're leaving on the table by selling books for 50¢ each, but I've never communicated this to them directly.

Book Arbitrage

Buy books on eBay cheaply and sell higher on Amazon. Search for "book lot." The biggest opportunities are in the lots too big to ship, which are available for pickup only. I have eBay email me anytime an auction goes up in the category "Books > Wholesale & Book Lots > More than 500" within 200 miles of my house. Disclaimer: Screen heavily. Most books lots are other sellers trying to unload their castaways, or are otherwise picked over. Ask a lot of questions to be sure you're not inheriting someone else's problems.

Friends of the Library
In addition to FoL sales, you can shortcut directly to the organization. Make a pitch to the director to start selling online for a commission. These organizations are generally run by retirees who have no idea how to sell online. There are also stories of libraries selling an entire book sale's worth of books to resellers for a lump sum to avoid the labor of holding a sale.

Rummage Sale & Church Book Sales
These tend to be less publicized than library book sales, and thus more fruitful (*see sidebar*).

Colleges
The person who has a consistent way to get her hands on large amounts of sellable textbooks rules the bookselling world. Towards the end of each semester, I'll post signs offering to buy textbooks the bookstores won't buy back. Then I arrange for anyone who inquires to meet at a designated time and place. I choose a parking lot on campus, where I'll make my buying decisions on the spot and offer cash for each book.

Recyclers
Approach local recyclers and ask if they will sell you their books. Offer to pay more than the pulp value. According to Adam Bertman, author of *How to Source Used Books,* recyclers only receive $15 to $50 per ton for paper pulp, making higher offers palatable. Do a walk-in or call them and offer to buy books by the "gaylord"(industry term for something approximating a pallet).

UNCONVENTIONAL SOURCING

A list of sources that have been profitable for me and are under-reported or rarely mentioned:

Retail Book Chain Bargain Bins
I have made good money from the bargain sections of Barnes & Noble as well as chains that deal in whole or in part with remainder books, like Books-

A-Million. Depending on the season, Books-A-Million can have thousands of titles for one or two dollars. These are books that do not do well on the brick-and-mortar level, but can have a demand on Amazon.

Barnes & Noble's bargain section is often overlooked because you're spending more than thrift store prices and the margins are generally lower. The advantage is that you can buy multiples of each copy. This past Christmas, I bought a stack of Jack London collections published by Barnes & Noble Books for $10 and sold them for $80. Recently, I bought 10 copies of *Social Intelligence* in hardcover for approximately $4.50 each. With no Amazon or FBA offers, I sold all 10 for $20 each. Note that bargains surge in the weeks after Christmas.

Dollar Stores (The ones where everything really is a dollar.)
Chains like Dollar Tree and smaller local dollar stores often stock dollar books. You will find many new books ranked better than 1 million that have no non-FBA value, but also have no competing FBA offers, thereby allowing you to set the price. Occasionally you'll find books that have value even in the non-FBA market. Last month I bought 20 copies of a book that is consistently ranked above 100,000 and sells for $25. I'll do the circuit of dollar stores in my city and consistently bring home 30 or more books in a few hours. It's modest, but worth my time.

Independent Bookstores
This is not an oft-cited profit source, perhaps because many consider it distasteful, a cross-pollinating of worlds that are seemingly at odds. In fact, this is an instance where offline and online sellers meet each other's needs in harmony.

Many bookstores do not sell online, and almost none have *all* their inventory listed. They may list only the collectible books, or books priced over $25, but rarely will they list everything.

Two weeks ago, a new bookstore opened up two blocks from my home. I went in five minutes before closing, found the business section, and scanned six books. Four were each priced at $7, had a rank better than 400,000, and showed a net payout of over $20. In a few minutes, I had made nearly $100.

Another bookstore near my house has rotating sales on various sections. My first visit, I found all psychology titles were 50% off. I spent $350 on books costing $2 to $15, and didn't come close to exhausting the potential. I repeat this every time a profitable category goes on sale at this store.

A note on scanning in bookstores: Be discreet (read: invisible). Many, if not most, bookstore owners would take great offense to seeing someone scanning their inventory. It is part a perception that this is an affront to their intelligence and skill as a bookseller (implying their books are undervalued); part the bitterness that online bookselling is destroying their business (they're right).

These are legitimate grievances, but misguided. In fact, by nature of the fact that you're turning a profit off their inventory, your books are selling for more than theirs, and so you probably aren't driving their prices down or selling to their market. And to scan is not to say they don't know the value of their books, it is just an example of a market differential; you're buying from one market and selling to another market, one where you can command a higher price.

The true reason I think bookstores are overlooked is explained in more detail in the "Blind Spots" chapter. Thrift stores and library sales have lulled everyone into a

Buying Book Sale Leftovers?

Some sellers arrange to buy book-sale leftovers, mine them for books with FBA-value, and discard the rest. I've purchased several book sale leftover lots myself. What I learned is this: there is almost no point to purchasing book sale leftovers from a sale that you can attend yourself — especially when most sales end with bag sales or huge discounts on the final day. It takes vastly less time to scan books at the sale than it does to arrange transport for thousands of books and scan them at home.

Transporting and then sorting thousands of books will take at least an entire workday, and the process makes you feel like you've accidentally gotten yourself a real job. Save yourself the time and spend a fraction of it scanning books at the sale.

In every instance of purchasing library sale leftovers, I bought 3,000 to 5,000 books — and extracted less than $250 of profit from each. And for that profit, I spent 12 to 16 hours making multiple trips to and from the library, scanning, packing, and shipping the crumbs of value I extracted. Not worth it.

There are only two scenarios where would I advise buying leftovers:

- Sales you were not able to attend.
- Sales where prices exceed $1.

comfortable form of sleepwalking, where no book can cost more than $2, and anything more is an unthinkable outrage.

You can also find out if the store sells online. If not, this is an opportunity to speak with the owner about a consignment arrangement, where you handle their online sales for a cut of the profit. This is especially attractive to stores that have more inventory than they have room for.

University Surplus Stores & Auctions

Many universities (including the one near me) have on-campus surplus stores. These are nearly always unadvertised, and sometimes open only to students and faculty. They also never stop anyone who walks in the door, and I've never been asked for ID. Every store I've visited has discarded textbooks, sometimes in the thousands, either loose or in pallets. I've never seen any indication the books are picked over by other sellers, or that any other sellers have picked up on this lucrative source.

Next are the surplus auctions. Want a pallet of books for a penny? Those are the stories that come out of university surplus auctions. All universities have tons of surplus, and all have a means of liquidating it. Some now do it online. Some, as said, have an on-campus store. Usually, they do a regular auction. The search term "[school name] surplus auction" should give you the answers. Or call up the surplus department of your local university and ask how they sell their surplus.

Craigslist

As part of my morning ritual, I do a quick scan of Craigslist in these categories: Books, CD/DVD/VHS, and Garage Sales. Right off the top, the Books section is 98% people trying to sell John Grisham hardbacks for $10. I disregard any listing advertising individual books and hone in on the lots, such as listings saying "hundreds of books," "tons of books," or "storage unit full of books."

I do the same under CDs/DVD/VHS.

Recently I purchased a collection of 250 history books from a woman who had inherited them from her father and just wanted to be rid of them. I paid $100 and the listing prices for the books totaled over $2,000.

People on Craigslist are especially prone to being talked down on price. I never offer—and rarely pay—the price in the ad.

Additionally, I regularly post ads under "wanted" and "books," offering to buy book collections of 500 or more. Most of the responses you receive will not be fruitful, but you will get the occasional person cleaning out his grandfather's attic who will give you 1,000 military history books for $50.

Freecycle

Sign up at *Freecycle.com*. This will unleash a barrage of emails to your inbox everyday for people giving away everything from floorboards to inflatable swimming pools. I keep an eye open for books, VHS, and CDs. Occasionally you will see interesting non-media items being given away that are FBA-profitable. Tip: If your email service offers it as an option, have any email that doesn't contain the words "books", "CD," or "VHS" sent straight to the trash folder.

Dumpster Diving

I love dumpster diving. If you're thinking something like *If it had value, why would someone throw it away?*, you're asking the wrong question. Which is fine. More for me.

The lord king god of all dumpster expeditions is the dorms of any large university at the end of the semester. Why would students throw away valuable books? There's no good answer, but it doesn't mean they don't do it. A lot. Just do the equation: Person who has all bills paid for by parents + having to fit an entire dorm room into a 2001 Honda Civic = tons of lucrative trash.

(A couple months ago, I hoped to find the mothership of all book dumpsters by taking a small road trip to one of the biggest wholesale book warehouses in the world. I was dismayed to find a row of large trash compactors in lieu of more accessible dumpsters.)

Other fruitful dumpster diving locations:

- Used bookstores (especially the local chains and larger stores that can afford to throw away books.)
- Thrift stores (try it — you'll be surprised.)
- Libraries (I've found two books in local library dumpsters that I've sold for $100 & up. And if you want thousands of books you might extract some FBA value from, go behind the library the day after a book sale ends.)

Overstock Stores

There are multiple discount, remainder, and overstock stores in my area that have book and DVD sections. These are stores that you find through sheer determination and mileage, and at first glance don't appear to be fruitful — but keep looking. Generally the prices are higher, but I always find gems. Yesterday I purchased a shrink-wrapped art book for $20 that will sell for $100.

BULK BUYING VS. NOT

Many believe it is not possible to make good money without sourcing in bulk. Yet I have gotten within stone's-throw of a six-figure income largely through the "single-sourcing" approach. It can be done. The largest factor here is the number of sources you can locate locally.

That said, I encourage you to break through to wholesale sourcing and non-media as soon as you are comfortable.

To recap, here are a few of the wholesale sources we've covered (I'll define "wholesale sourcing" as any source that brings you 500 or more items at a time):

- Thrift store surplus
- Recyclers
- Auctions
- Book lots on eBay
- Craigslist
- Consignment deals with Friends of the Library, bookstores, etc.

Notes on buying blind

A few notes on making offers for large lots before being able to look them over:

- Find out all you can about the origins of the books: You should offer much less for the discards from a nursing home library than a deceased history professor.
- When buying blind, keep your costs to 1 to 2 cents a book or a dollar or two a box. Adjust downward for high-risk factors, upwards for high-yield.
- Always ask the seller if they sell on Amazon, or the books have been picked over by another seller.

ADVANCED SOURCING: TIPS & STRATEGIES NO ONE ELSE WILL TELL YOU

8

THE ZEN OF BOOK SHOPPING
CUTTING SHOPPING TIME DOWN BY 95%
WHAT NOT TO BUY
SOURCING PRINCIPLES
BUYING FORMULAS
BLIND SPOTS: MONEY IN THE SHADOWS
THE PSYCHOLOGY OF THE HUNT

YOUR SUBCONSCIOUS SCANNER: THE ZEN OF BOOK SHOPPING

This week I was in a thrift store I'd never visited, in a town an hour away. There is a sort of radar you develop as a bookseller that allows you to detect other buyers in any given environment from across the room, and I knew from 50 yards away there was another seller in the store. I ducked behind a rack of scarves and did some surveillance.

She had a setup I had never seen before, imported straight from some third-world technology black hole. Something with the makeup of a child's TV tray was placed across the top of her cart. On it was a circa-2004 laptop, connected to a massive barcode scanner, the type you might have seen at a Sears in 1986. The woman was positioned by the romance novels, where she was scanning each one into her Mesopotoic system. She moved through each Harlequin title, scanning, looking at the computer screen, and putting the books back on the shelf.

While it's probably unhealthy, I tend to deem every bookseller in range of my house as a threat. Two things told me this woman was not a threat:

1. Her equipment: It was really archaic.
2. Her lack of methodology: I occasionally sell Christian romance at a profit, but the percentage of used Harlequin romance novels that can be sold profitably have to be a fraction of a percent. This woman was scanning everything, indiscriminately.

At any large thrift store, you could literally spend an entire eight-hour day scanning every book. I'm going to lay out a formula that will get you through a whole store in a fraction of that time.

The bookseller, for the sake of efficiency, has to develop a subconscious filtering system. You need a formula that will allow you to size up books at a glance and decide which are worth scanning and which are almost certainly without value. Then, from the few books that pass this test, the scanner will reveal what goes in your cart.

A lot of this filtering mechanism is intuitive and defies breaking down into parts. Often I'm unable to isolate why I think a book is worth money, my subconscious has just done a complicated calculation based on many variables and makes its judgment. To the extent that I understand it, this chapter will attempt to teach you this formula.

The accuracy of your subconscious filtering mechanism determines how much money you make. And its accuracy will increase over time. It is a muscle that will be flexed the more you go out, scan, and take mental notes on the patterns that emerge.

You don't have enough time to scan every book. Scouting programs can take five to ten seconds per scan to load, and you have many better things to do than go through 500 hardcover titles for the one that will net you $7.

This is a list of every common book category, and how to decide if you should scan:

Recent editions of timeless classics

I will buy paperback editions of timeless classics often without even scanning, because I know demand is steady, and these titles do well with Amazon Prime customers. Newer editions of books like *The Great Gatsby* and *Grapes of Wrath*, philosophy titles by Neitzche and Plato, and enduring non-fiction books like *Think and Grow Rich* and *Getting to Yes*.

When considering these books, ask yourself this: Are they recent editions, or can I list them as recent editions without offending the customer? (See the chapter on "Black Hat Tricks" for more.)

Textbooks

I will usually scan most textbooks, because when they're valuable, they can be very valuable, and worth the extra time. I will skip books that are clearly over a decade old or custom editions for small schools.

Hardcover fiction

This is the one category everyone can agree on — *skip hardcover fiction*. It's a question of how much your time is worth, because I can promise that out of 1000 hardcover fiction titles, you will find *something* you can sell. But here are the facts: Hardcover fiction has an *extremely* short shelf life. If a hardcover fiction title is ever hot at all, it is hot for a split second, and then falls off the deep end of the sales rank ladder — never to return.

If you choose to scan hardcover fiction, you're probably still making more than minimum wage. I choose FBA as a tool to decrease time spent working.

And by this measure, hardcover fiction is not an efficient use of my time.

Unlike non-fiction, it is impossible to gauge potential value based on subject matter. What this means is, there is no way to look at a fiction book and make any snap assessment of its potential for value. If you're going to scan hardcover fiction, you just have to scan everything. When you combine this with how few hardback fiction titles are worth anything, this is the lowest-yield book category there is.

There will always be exceptions. Several months ago I'd spent two hours at a library book sale and had almost run out of books to scan. While I waited for a friend to finish shopping, I wandered to the last corner of the sale I hadn't touched: the hardcover fiction. The first book I picked up caught my eye because it appeared self-published, which can make for some interesting prose. This particular title was a survivalist tale with a libertarian message. After flipping the pages I scanned it on a whim and found it was ranked 200,000 and selling for $350.

When they are grouped together, I will do a quick once-over to look for books with a more modern design in newer condition, indicating they may still be sellable. I may scan a few, but generally I'm on to the next thing.

Diet books
One of the least profitable categories. I will almost never scan these unless I recognize something as a recent best seller. This is among the most faddy of genres — big one minute, gone the next. Then the market gets saturated with used copies and demand falls off a cliff.

Books on fleeting news stories
High profile murder cases, momentary celebrities, flash-in-the-pan news stories: These are the books that sell tons of copies quickly, and that everyone is unloading their copies of six months later.

Biographies & autobiographies
If the person was a here-today-gone-tomorrow temporary celebrity, there is very little chance his or her book is sellable. It is even less likely when the book is hardcover.

Books on or by more timeless celebrities, or biographies of bands who have more timeless appeal, are worth scanning. Examples of recent biographies

I've sold are books on Eric Clapton, The Eagles, and Kerouac. Exceptions to this are books on presidents published by major publishing houses — there is almost always a glut of these titles. Altogether a very hit-or-miss category.

Romance books
Skip. The occasional Christian romance title is excepted. (Do you see Long Tail Theory at work here? Niche appeal = potential for profit.)

Mass market paperbacks
These are the small, romance-novel-sized titles printed in mass quantities for quick consumption. They are quickly obsolete and forgotten. And for whatever reason, many (if not most) of the barcodes don't come up on Amazon when scanned.

Travel books
Unless it's the newest edition, the Fodors and Frommers and similar mass market mainstream travel titles drop in sales rank faster than almost any other category. Seriously, it's worse than hardcover fiction. Most travel books are ranked worse than 2 million. Scan for titles that look recent, or for anything niche (e.g. *Ghost Tours of Nashville*). Ignore the rest.

Exceptions: Some of the more down-to-earth and esoteric travel imprints (like the Rough Guides series) tend to hold their value better than other travel books.

Religious books
This is a strange category with a Wild West feel. It is so vast, with so many titles and authors crowding the genre, that it is almost impossible to apply a buying formula. There are no apparent patterns to what people who consume religious books will buy. I scan almost anything that looks like it was printed in the last 15 years. This is a consistent and profitable category.

Religious books seems to have the highest percentage of titles in the $5 to $10 range.

Health books
As distinct from the Diet category, there can be a lot of profit here. The books that tend to hold the most Amazon value are progressive titles that cover more "fringe" (a.k.a. long tail) topics like Eastern medicine, homeopathy, raw foodism, and veganism. I would purchase any book in the latter two subjects without even scanning, as more than 90% of the time they will have value.

Again, if it's hardcover, it has to appear in new condition or be written for a niche audience for me to scan.

Recent sales in this category to illustrate: A book on naturopathic medicine I sold for $325, and *Radical Self-Defense*, a natural healing title I sold for $60.

Parenting, pregnancy, & childcare books

There are a lot of trends in this genre. Generally, look for titles that appear by their layout to be published in the last few years.

Children's books

It takes a lot of enthusiasm for me to go near these, but I know of people who consider this category to be an overlooked goldmine.

Here's what you're going to see when you approach a shelf of children's books: thousands of small books in total disarray, most without even a spine by which to judge their contents. It's total chaos, and the gems are always in short supply.

Here are a few types of books that often find their way into the children's books and frequently have value:

- Manga (Sorters see "comics" and toss them on the kids shelf.)
- How-to books (Subjects like how to play piano for kids and similar books often have value.)
- Grade school textbooks (These can sell for more than you'd think.)

Like most non-hardcover books, I scan anything that looks new or potentially collectible.

Cookbooks

Another "scanner beware" category. I'll give a glance for anything related to natural foods and move on.

Business books

My favorite. The less sensational and snake-oil-salesman the book appears, the better the chances it has value. Books like *How to Be a Real Estate Mogul with no Money Down* is less likely to have value than *High-Frequency Trading: A Practical Guide to Algorithmic Strategies and Trading Systems*. The former title people feel cheated by and get rid of resulting in a used market glut. The latter has timeless information that retains value to people over the years, which they are more likely to hold onto and assign value to. Another distinction: The latter has appeal to more sophisticated and affluent online shoppers — exactly your Amazon Prime demographic.

Books offering valuable information that is *not* time sensitive or obsolete; that are *not* based around a business "personality" (i.e. Jim Cramer, Robert Kiyosaki); and that *don't* have a flashy "buy me now and regret me later" title are most likely to be profitable.

The winning formula for business titles: Books that fit the above criteria, in new condition, published on a smaller press, that don't have a sensationalized title, and have been published relatively recently.

University press titles

Books published by any "University of (fill in the blank) Press", or by schools under any name (Stanford, Harvard, Oxford) are books you definitely want to give attention to. Why? They almost always pass the Long Tail Test (see section of the same name). University presses publish books with extreme niche appeal (e.g. *The Fur Farms of Alaska* on University of Alaska Press) for which no competing titles exist. University press titles tend to remain in people's personal collections as long-term reference titles, and are not quickly deemed to be obsolete or out of vogue. They also tend to be more expensive. This is the perfect checklist for online value.

You will find a large percentage of university press titles having used price values on Amazon of $15 and up, with sales ranks of 2 million and worse. Should you buy it? Most people would avoid any book ranked this poorly. I'll buy them every time, *if* they pass my Long Tail Test.

About a year ago I purchased a book titled *Not Just Any Medical School: The Science, Practice, and Teaching of Medicine at the University of Michigan, 1850-1941* on the University of Michigan Press. Rank: 2.5 million. Most booksellers would dismiss it immediately based on the rank alone. But that doesn't tell the whole story. I knew there was virtually no chance there was another book on this subject. I also knew that someday, someone would want this title. And I would be right there when they did. I sold the book in 6 months for a $40 profit. I've repeated this story over a thousand times.

Computer books

If you're not schooled in computer trends, you won't be able to decipher how relevant most computer books are based on title. Layout is also another poor gauge—most computer books have a minimalist layout that prevent easily telling if a book was published yesterday or fifteen years ago.

To make it even harder, when a computer book becomes obsolete, it *really* becomes obsolete. This is another category where books often fall off the sales rank cliff and never return for a single sale ever again.

The good news: Computer books are generally expensive and if you find one that is still relevant, you may have a score. I scan anything that reasonably looks like it could have been published in the last ten years, covers a subject that will maintain its relevance, or is so esoteric I can't understand it. Recent example: *Low Tech Hacking: Street Smarts for Security Professionals.*

Paperback fiction

Scan anything in new condition.

Scan anything that looks published in the last 5-ish years.

Scan any of the classics in any condition, if they appear to be recent editions.

The rule of thumb with fiction versus non is that the opposite rules apply. Most fiction with any value is published by major publishing houses. Small press fiction rarely builds an audience.

MISCELLANEOUS PRINCIPLES FOR BOOK SCANNING

There is some sort of inverse relationship between how ostentatious a book's layout is and how well it holds its value. Any book with arrows and bright colors and layout features that yell at you is likely to be a penny book sixty days after its release.

Conversely, a minimalist design indicates professionalism, arcane subject matter, and a target audience that is willing to pay for what the book is offering. A book that doesn't need to oversell its value likely has a lot of it.

This principle also applies to titles and subtitles. A title that oversells its point indicates content with low worth, and consequently, low Amazon value. If

I see any book titled *The Get Rich Quick Guide to* _____, *How to Make Millions With* _____, or anything on getting rich through real estate, I'll usually pass. (By the way, this is the reason I didn't subtitle this book *How I (Almost) Made Six Figures My First Year With FBA*.)

As a rule of thumb, hardcovers in every genre generally have less value than paperbacks (textbooks and scholarly books excluded). It's counterintuitive, but so it is.

And the biggest one of all: If it looks like it was published in the last couple years, scan. If the design looks contemporary, it has a much greater chance of having value.

The importance of your internal book value calculator

The very day I sit to write this section, I passed a garage sale coming back from the store and didn't have my scanner. I pulled over and knew at a glance that it was a goldmine. There were hundreds of university press books on astronomy and physics, and several more boxes of brand new books on eastern religion—categories that are generally profitable. I bought forty books for a dollar each, relying solely on my "internal scanner," and brought them home.

Yes.   No.

Of the forty, thirty-four were books I would have bought if I had my scanner with me—an 85% accuracy rate.

Final note on categories

There are books of value in every category, format, and era. There will be no shortage of protest cries from countless booksellers about every single thing I've written here. This guide assumes that you have a rich, varied life and wish to maximize your profit-to-time ratio—not to extract every last penny of profit from the bottom of Goodwill's barrel.

Be comfortable knowing that you're going to miss profitable items everywhere you go. But your work day just decreased by 75%. And there is nothing more important than your time.

BUYING FORMULA FOR MOVIES & MUSIC

DVDs
If it's sealed, scan it.

If it's not sealed, there is one paramount rule: If you haven't heard of it, scan it. If you have heard of it, don't. Unless demand is very, very high or a release is very new, there is little money in big Hollywood DVDs and VHS. The market is saturated with used copies. Even as an FBA seller, it's hard to scrape a profit out of a used copy of any mainstream film.

There are exceptions (like box sets), but generally the rule holds.

The opportunity lies in the rest of the DVDs: the instructional yo yo DVDs, documentaries on the North Dakota skateboarding scene, and doing yoga while pregnant. Band documentaries, improving your golf game, and dumpster diving are among the one zillion subjects that have their own DVDs that people will pay a premium for.

A few of the DVD subjects I will almost always buy without even scanning include: golf, magic, and pretty much any instructional video on anything weird.

Note: In 2014, DVDs became a "gated category." Meaning: You must get approved to sell DVDs on Amazon. Sellers who have not sold any DVDs prior to September 2014 *must get approval from Amazon to sell <u>any</u> DVDs. Sellers who <u>have</u> sold DVDs before September 2014 only have to approve to sell DVDs that have a manufacturer's suggested retail price of $25 or more. Currently, not a lot of sellers get approved to sell all DVDs. Approval to sell DVDs with an MSRP under $25 is more common.*

Also note this does not mean you can't sell DVDs for over $25. Only those with an MSRP, which does not apply to the majority of DVDs on Amazon.

VHS

VHS is tougher, but scan anything sealed and anything you haven't heard of, and you'll come out of the store with enough profit to buy your own used VCR, at least.

Read the "Blind Spots" section for more on VHS, but it's worth repeating: You would be shocked at what people will pay for some VHS tapes at this point in the century. Certainly I was. I recently sold a sealed VHS for $89.99 that I bought at an overstock store for 50¢.

CDs

The music that seems to hold its value best is classical, jazz, and music of other genres typically favored by a more sophisticated, older audience. Those are always the first I go for when I'm at a sale or thrift store.

Like books, I'm also looking for anything weird: CDs by comedians I've never heard of, soundtracks for obscure 80s movies, and old hip hop.

And as with movies, I will scan anything that's sealed.

One thing: Don't plan to price higher than $3.99 above the lowest merchant fulfilled offers for all but the best-ranked titles. In my experience, Prime subscribers just aren't buying CDs in enough volume to make pricing any higher profitable.

ENDNOTES

This guide is not meant to prepare you for a hyper-evolved, post-scanner stage of your business in which you make major money on tech-free, blink-speed decisions. But it is intended to give you the knowledge to turn a six-hour thrift store visit into thirty minutes. This information will streamline the inventory-acquisition process, making for a more sustainable and profitable business.

TO BE OR NOT TO BE UNDER THE RADAR: A NOTE ON SECRECY

There are definitely two types of media sellers: Those who scan in the open without regard for witnesses, and those who work surreptitiously.

I am firmly in the latter camp for two reasons:

1.   It invites competition from customers. I live in a town where I own the used book market. Other than small, occasional hints, there appear to be no other scanners or booksellers. All editorializing on diversifying my business aside, if there was even one other person going to my spots my income would take a huge hit. Scanning items openly is a big advertisement that reads: "There is money being made here." (Non-media is another story because there are greater barriers to entry: specifically the need for more capital.) If one out of every thousand people who witnessed me at work started shopping my spots themselves—trouble. I take the threat seriously.

2.   It invites competition from stores. Scanning openly advertises that a store (from thrift store to overstock store) is leaving money on the table. Once that light bulb goes off, it may only be a matter of time before they start selling on Amazon. And a lot of stores are starting to do this.

It's just not worth it.

This is why I love the Scanfob versus the old school PDA & Socket scanner setup. A Scanfob makes it easy to scan with stealth. I affix mine with Velcro to the underside of my cell phone and it is barely perceptible.

A lot of sellers call this approach paranoia. I call it an investment in sustainability.

Sometimes, you'll get called out. I've been thrown out of a couple stores by owners or managers whose egos have taken a hit by my scanning, which they interpret as a neon sign reading, "You're too stupid to know what your merchandise is really worth."

You will also occasionally be asked by other customers what you're doing. I use the line I picked up in Susan Wells's e-book *Amazon 90-Day Experiment*:

"The scanner tells me if the book is already in my inventory." Short, simple, and totally uninteresting to almost anyone who asks.

Just please don't ever tell anyone that you have a magic tool that tells you what the books are worth (which you do).

BLIND SPOTS: PROFIT IN THE SHADOWS

The successful Amazon seller is always looking in places their competition isn't. This chapter is about making money off what the other guys consider to be of no value, too much work—or what they never notice at all.

Blind Spot I: Cult of the $1 Book

Three years ago I had moved to a new city and attended the bi-annual library book sale. I was selling on Amazon casually at the time, and was easily deterred by competition. I entered the sale and stopped cold. Looking down every one of the fifteen aisles I saw at least three people with scanners in a full Tasmanian devil-style frantic trance—scanning, tossing books, elbowing each other, running around... I wanted no part.

Through a side door I found the "Special Books Room." These were books the library had deemed to be of exceptional value and were each individually priced from $5 to $20. The room was much smaller, but still had 5,000 to 10,000 books. Noticeably absent was a single person with a scanner.

I took comfort in a bookseller-free zone and began scanning. In short time I had filled several boxes of $5 and $10 books for which my scanner was showing at least a 300% profit.

I was bracing myself for the Tasmanian devil invasion, expecting them to migrate into that room once the sale progressed. But they never came. I scanned for several hours, leaving with over 150 books. I returned the next day and spent several more hours. By the end of the sale I hadn't seen one person with a scanner even put their head in that room.

In those two days I spent over $1,000. There is no question I had invested more than any other bookseller there. I also made more—a lot more. And I did it by working inside a blindspot.

Most Amazon media sellers are in a trance, living under the illusion they are eternally entitled to pay no more than a dollar for anything. Above this amount, there is a tacit belief that profits vanish. The world of books over one or two dollars is a strange netherland where they dare not tread, as it would bring the risk of spending more than 50¢ on inventory for something they call a business. God forbid.

Shortly after the aforementioned book sale, I honed in on a small chain of used bookstores and made decent money buying their underprice textbooks; reference books; and long tail business, investing, and science books at full sticker price. The store had a dollar-book clearance section, where I would regularly see sellers with scanners hunched over, picking up the last person's crumbs. All the while, I was one aisle over making more money then all of them combined and with zero competition. The best place to hide, as they say, is in plain sight.

Today I live in another city. And my most profitable inventory source is a store that charges a flat $5 per book. I consistently spend $300 or more per visit and, of course, always triple my money. And, if I may belabor the point, in its long history, that store has probably never seen another human being with a scanner.

"You have to spend money to make money." Enjoy a competition-free zone in the realm of $3+ books, the bookseller's greatest blind spot.

Blind Spot II: "New" books

By "new", I mean pre-owned books in new condition. The high-volume booksellers, who will make up the majority of your most ruthless competition, can't grade the condition of individual books accurately. They process thousands of books per day, and many by default grade everything as "good". One thing they rarely do is list a book as new condition. They are volume sellers focused on getting the books out the door, not taking a careful assessment of every item's condition.

Check any title where there is a glut of used FBA offers. You will find there is vastly less competition in the New category. This opens up territory with little competition: sourcing pre-owned books in flawless, new condition condition that can be listed as new.

Blind Spot III: VHS

As of this writing, we are in the middle of a massive VHS purge, much like we saw with vinyl in the late 1980s. Thrift stores have an unmanageable glut of VHS tapes and can't sell enough to keep up with donations. I frequently see shelves set aside for VHS stacked two-deep and spilling over onto other shelves as stores try to find the space. A lot of VHS just end up in the dumpster (go back there and look).

For years, I never considered scanning VHS tapes, simply because I didn't believe anyone still bought VHS. After reading Steve Lindhorst's book *Amazon Quick and Dirty Guide II: Leftover Gold*, I began leaving every thrift store and rummage sale with three or four tapes. Using the rule "If you haven't heard of it, scan it," I quickly built up an inventory of VHS. And I started to watch them sell, steadily.

Some VHS are very collectible. A lot of films, documentaries, etc. never made it to DVD. The only place to see them is on VHS. These can command major money.

The following films—many of which feature A-list stars—were never released on DVD and have serious resale value:

> *1986*
> *A New Leaf*
> *Brewster McCloud*
> *Captain EO* (Micheal Jackson)
> *Deadman's Curve* (Jan and Dean)
> *Decline of Western Civilization* (whole trilogy)

Dudes
Flim Flam Man
Last Summer
Legend Of Lizzie Borden
Let It Be (Beatles)
Lisztomania
Mr. Boogedy
No Holds Barred (Hulk Hogan)
Queen of Hearts
Rad
So Big
Song of the South
The Last Movie (Dennis Hopper)
The Wild Life
The World's Greatest Sinner
Treasure Island (1990)
Twilights Last Gleaming

Today I have just short of 300 VHS tapes in my inventory. In the last 30 days, I have grossed $412 in VHS sales.

> ## Media Blind Spots: The Cumulative Effect
>
> A short list of used media blind spots:
>
> - Books ranked worse than 1 million
> - VHS
> - CDs
>
> These categories are easily dismissed as "not worth the time," yet each one represents a small amount of monthly revenue. Together, these over-looked items bring me over $1000 per month.

This is another example of how crucial it is to have numerous revenue streams within the FBA framework. Specifically, by including the small niche-category sales that don't provide an income on their own, but which add up to create significant profit.

Blind Spot III: CDs

This is another blindspot worth your time at any sale or thrift store. Like VHS, we are in the middle of a CD purge, and this is a micro-gold rush worth getting in on.

Although iTunes is killing the CD, not many people realize there are some artists who won't sell their music on iTunes. Their protest move is your profit. Anyone who wants their music has no choice but to buy the CD. When I see these artists CDs, I will put them in my cart without even scanning:

AC/DC
Black Sabbath (albums Ozzy sang on)

Def Leppard
Kid Rock
The Smiths
Tool

Blind Spot IV: Covered barcodes

A lot of stores (who clearly aren't acting with Amazon sellers in mind) put their price sticker right over the book's barcode. These places are often the most lucrative simply because few Amazon sellers have the guts to peel back or scratch off a store's price tag. Is it vandalism? I'm not sure, but I know it's win-win because the more price stickers I remove, the more I buy.

My single most lucrative book source, which I referenced earlier, covers all their bar codes with price stickers I must scratch off one by one. They haven't confronted me yet.

The Book Blacklist

As a cheat sheet for very beginners, these are books you'll find everywhere that (almost) never have value in used condition. Avoiding these used book staples will save you a lot of time.

- *Chicken Soup for the Soul* series
- Mass market fiction authors: Danielle Steel, John Grisham, Scott Turow, etc.
- Time-Life books
- Reader's Digest books
- Romance novels
- Anything 6.5 x 4" (mass market paperbacks)

119

Blind Spot V: Books without barcodes

With these you must enter the ISBN into your pricing program manually. Most sellers aren't going to do this, which gives you an advantage—*if* you have a formula for determining the "possibly valuable" from the "definitely not." The Long Tail Test will act as a guide.

Blind Spot VI: Books ranked worse than 1 million

Poor-rank-phobia and all facets of this subject are covered heavily in the chapter on buying strategy, and I will not burden you with much redundancy here. To recap what we learned in that chapter:

- Nearly all booksellers do not know how to interpret what a sales rank of 1 million means.
- Nearly all the available literature on selling books online tells you to stay away from books ranked worse than 1 million (often, you're told to stay away from books ranked worse than 500,000).
- Nearly all booksellers heed this advice. The ones who don't are unable to distinguish between a niche title ranked 2 million (sellable) and a wholly obsolete title ranked 2 million (unsellable).

All of this comes together to create a massive blind spot.

And, it creates a massive advantage for those who arm themselves with

Shutting down the sale

Often I will show up at a sale that has books, but is not exclusively books. If the books are in profit-rich categories and I know at a glance there is money there, I'll always attempt to make an offer for the entire lot.

I find the person in charge and ask her to put a price on the entire lot. Because of the dazzling effect of a large number and the pressure of a time constraint, you can often get an entire lot for less than you would have doing it piecemeal. It's a quirk of human psychology: People are much more mesmerized by a $100 bill than 300 people each handing them $1.

Last weekend I purchased 250 books in the profit-rich "New Age" category for $20, mid-sale at a Unitarian Church fund raiser. I extracted 40 books of value that would have otherwise cost me $1 each.

knowledge, understand what sales rank means, and know how to identify a book with a long tail, niche demand.

THE SCIENCE OF SOURCING INVENTORY

Ultimately how much money you make comes down to the quality of your sources.

Successful booksellers often have sources they guard like their young. Everyone has a secret source (or five) that are their bread and butter. I do, and I'll never talk.

No one buys a book that just tells them to "think like a bookseller." You want hard how-to instruction. So with that part out of the way, a little psychology...

Media Hunter's Third Eye: Your Reticular Activation System (RAS)

There is something almost supernatural that happens when you commit yourself to a purpose. That which you assign value to, you start to see... everywhere. And this isn't Wayne Dyer mysticism. It's called your Reticular Activation System (RAS).

The RAS is a part of your brain that processes all sensory input and passes along to the conscious mind only that which you have told it is relevant. Ever learned a new word, and then suddenly you hear the word everywhere? Or bought a Prius, and suddenly every third car is a Prius? This is you Reticlular Activation System at work.

When you wholly commit yourself to the mission of building a massive inventory of books and media, you begin to see them everywhere. I have so many unconventional sources in my area that would have been lost in the white-scenery-noise of the big city had my RAS not locked in on them with its laser beam focus. These include:

- A used book table inside a small grocery store
- A used book cart at the university library
- A used hardware store that also sells used books

Every one of these would likely have passed into my field of vision prior to committing myself to bookselling, yet would not have consciously registered.

The wrong question to ask before entering the business is: *Where can I buy used books in my town?*

Your RAS hasn't been alerting you to them yet.

Step through that door and you will begin to see books and media everywhere.

SHIPPING EVERYTHING TO AMAZON

9

WHAT NOT TO SEND TO AMAZON (NOTHING)
LABELING ITEMS
FREE BOXES
PACKING
THE CHEAPEST SHIPPING IN THE ROOM
CREATING A SHIPMENT
GOING TO THE UPS STORE
PUTTING YOUR FEET UP

WHEN SHOULD I NOT SHIP TO AMAZON?

First decision: What inventory goes to FBA, and what should you keep in your closet to sell merchant fulfilled?

The dominant sentiment among FBA sellers is: don't ship a book to Amazon if it's ranked worse than 1 million. A lot of sellers will cap it at 500,000. Why? I have no idea.

First, a book ranked 1 million is not as poor-selling as it sounds. As I cover in the chapter on sales rank, a book ranked 1 million could have sold as recently as ten days ago.

Let's do some math: FBA storage for the average paperback costs just over 1¢ a month, or 14¢ a year. If you're storing books ranked 1.9 million and valued no less than $25, let's just say that book sells once a year. You'll net approximately $19 off that $25 book. By that math, if the book sells anytime in the next 135 years, you will still make money.

Why don't people ship everything to FBA? There is no reason you shouldn't be sending books ranked 5 million to Amazon. If you send in 500 of these extreme long tail books, and only *one* of them sells a year (an improbably low figure), you're still coming out ahead.

You can greatly limit the chances of a book never selling by applying the Long Tail Test (see chapter 4, on buying strategy). If an item passes the test, ship it to Amazon and rest easy knowing that one day, the right buyer will come along and that book will sell.

If you do choose to sell some of your inventory merchant-fulfilled, and want to go on vacation, not a problem. If you activate your vacation setting while you go to Fiji for a month, only your merchant-fulfilled titles (if any) go inactive. All your FBA inventory will continue to make you money.

As for my personal criteria for selling an item FBA, I will send in a book ranked if it meets the following criteria:

1. It's worth money.

So yes, I ship in everything. Going to the post office is *so* 2008.

Personally, I find going to the post office once a week with a $6 book to be a sub-optimal use of time. So I'll ship everything to Amazon and let FBA do its magic. I'm unconcerned if it sells this week, this month, or even this year. It's safe in Amazon's hands, and I'm happy to give them a cut to not have to think about my copy of *Punk Rock: An Oral History*.

BORING BUT NECESSARY: LABELING ITEMS

The first step in sending a shipment to Amazon is to label each item.

Your listing interface (Amazon, ScanPower, or something else) will generate an FBA barcode that you place over the item's original barcode. At the warehouse, Amazon will identify your products by this label. When your UPS package arrives at the FBA warehouse, the FBA sticker for every item will be scanned, telling Amazon's system what is in its warehouse.

You print the label after scanning in and creating a listing for your book (again, via your listing program, or Amazon's interface). This is usually the last step before placing the item in the box and shipping it to Amazon.

Amazon asks that you place the sticker completely over the item's barcode, to prevent the handler at the FBA warehouse from accidentally scanning the wrong barcode.

I'm actually surprised there are not more complaints from customers about stickers on their items, especially books (although these complaints do happen). There is nothing in the buying or checkout process that mentions this detail, which I would expect Amazon's princess-complex-afflicted customers to be offended by. But I've gotten very little negative feedback for FBA stickers.

The best preventative against this happening occasionally is to purchase stickers which are removed easily and without leaving residue. In my experience, the cheapest stickers are the opposite: removed only with a sandblaster.

Whatever labels you choose, I would advise against placing them on a "collectible" book—particularly titles for which the buyer paid significantly more to receive a copy in new condition. These buyers will be much more particular about the condition of their book, down to small details. I advise wrapping the book in bubble wrap (which you should do anyway) and placing the label on the outside.

THE ULTIMATE RENEWABLE (FREE) RESOURCE: BOXES

There is nothing in this country that is more abundantly free than cardboard boxes. Because every dumpster behind every strip mall is brimming with

them, I would never endorse paying for a cardboard box. If you ever reach the point in your business where you are sending more shipments to Amazon than local dumpsters can provide boxes for, then you know you've really made it. **That** is an incredibly successful FBA business.

I'm not even close, and I take a quick trip behind local businesses to source all my boxes.

HOW SHOULD YOU PACK YOUR BOXES?

Anyone who has shipped books via the most common book-shipping method—the USPS "Media Mail" rate—understands the turbulent journey those packages enjoy. Media Mail packages enjoy a wild ride and come out the other end much worse for the wear. The first time I sent a book Media Mail, the conversation went like this:

"Media Mail? You know we're going to treat this baby rough, don't you?"
"How rough?" I said.
"Rough."

My days using Media Mail are gone, but UPS doesn't exactly transport boxes via a network of angels and clouds. I've watched UPS workers toss my boxes ten feet into the truck, so you have to pack with a degree of rough handling in mind.

I separate all books by used and new. I toss used books loose into boxes, packing tightly but not concerning myself with Tetris-like precision.

With new books, I pack with greater care and in smaller boxes. I want them so tight there is no wiggle room. Any negative space I'll fill with plastic bags or newspaper to prevent movement during shipping.

Some hyper-cautious sellers will disagree, but I have not found it necessary to individually wrap books with bubble wrap before shipping, or otherwise give a huge amount of care to how I pack the boxes.

The sole exception is books I would deem "collectible". This would include genuinely collectible titles, and new books people have paid significantly more for than they otherwise would have for a used copy. In these instances, condition is paramount. They've paid a premium, and they want their money's worth. I will encase the book in several layers of bubble wrap and affix the label to the outside.

THE CHEAPEST SHIPPING IN THE ROOM: AMAZON / UPS PARTNERED SHIPPING

The first mental block I had to clear before making the switch to FBA was: "...but I have to pay to ship 1,500 books to Amazon." (This was my inventory at the time.) The preliminary math was painful, but I was estimating the cost to be somewhere in the range of $1,000. I trembled at the thought of a project that would include 70 boxes individually transported to the post office in a logistical exercise on par with Egyptian pyramid construction.

Of course, like every other conclusion I had rushed to about FBA, I was wrong. Amazon has a partnership with UPS that allows you to ship anything to an Amazon warehouse for between 20¢ to 60¢ per pound, depending on how far you are from the warehouse. That averages to about half the post office's already scandalously cheap Media Mail rate. This makes the price of shipping inventory so low it's a non-consideration.

CREATING A SHIPMENT

Here's how to create a shipment:

1. Scan the books into your listing software. Set price and condition, and upload to Amazon.
2. In your Amazon sellers account, click "Manage FBA Shipments" under "Inventory."
3. Select "Amazon Partnered Carrier."

4. Enter the number of boxes you are shipping in.
5. Estimate the weight of each box, and accept the charges.
6. Click "print box labels" to print the shipping labels. Seal each box.
7. Affix the shipping labels to the outside.

Your shipment is good to go.

GETTING THEM TO UPS

Once your boxes are packed, you have two options for getting them to Amazon.

1. Home pickup. For $5 a box, UPS will pick boxes up at your doorstep the
    next day ($6 for same-day pickup). This is a slick way to further automate

    your business. UPS also offers a variety of subscription type options
    ranging from $10 to $20 a week for multiple pickups. Each of these is a
    small price to pay for hugely streamlining your business.
2. UPS drop off. There are tons of places to drop off UPS packages. UPS
    stores are the obvious ones, but other options range from storage unit
    offices to Staples locations. Check out UPS.com for locations in your
    neighborhood. With your Amazon labels, the shipments are pre-paid,
    so give them to the UPS store attendant, get your receipt, and that's all
    there is to it.

CUTTING SHIPPING COSTS

The price of shipping books to Amazon is negligible, but there is one way to cut this cost. The price per pound drops after 50 pounds and 200 pounds. So the main way to cut shipping costs is to keep your *total* weight per shipment high, preferably over 200 pounds to get the best rate. Remember that a shipment can be made up of countless boxes.

YOU'RE DONE

And that's how you get your books to FBA. Now put up your feet and watch the money roll in.

Inside an FBA warehouse

You don't want a big blank thought bubble above your head while you're packing a box, trying to imagine its destination, and the path it will take from you to the customer's hands. To better understand and cement your relationship with FBA, I really advise watching videos taken inside an FBA warehouse.

Sharing links in books is somewhat annoying, but there is no way to capture the inner-workings of an FBA warehouse with words. Check out these videos:

http://www.youtube.com/watch?v=i6H7nfHjHtY

http://www.youtube.com/watch?v=5AVpuCMIk2A

http://www.guardian.co.uk/business/video/2009/nov/20/amazon-fulfilment-centre

http://www.amazonsellersupportblog.com/2010/07/take-a-look-inside-one-of-amazons-worldclass-fulfillment-centers-.html

YOU HAVE MADE A SALE: THE PART AMAZON TAKES CARE OF

10

TRACKING SALES

WHEN AN ITEM SELLS

This is the shortest chapter in the book because this is what you pay Amazon to do so you don't have to think about it.

Amazon doesn't tell you an item has sold until the credit card charge has cleared, and the order has been packed and is in the custody of UPS. Only then will you get an email from Amazon informing you that you've made a sale. This can sometimes be a few days from the placement of an order, so how do you know what you've sold in the meantime? Amazon rolls out the data in three stages:

First stop: "Orders" page.

The "Orders" page is the designer drug for the online mogul. Nothing stimulates your dopamine receptors quite like hitting refresh on the Orders page. Less disciplined sellers will find themselves checking this ten times a day. I'm not that bad, but I will often check in a couple times a day to scan for bigger sales.

This is not the simplest page to access, but if you really have to know when an item has sold right away, follow these steps:

Go to the "Manage Orders" page.
Click on "Advanced."
Check the box to show pending orders and sort by "Purchase Date."
Click "Search."

This will show you all orders that have been placed, shipped or not.

Second stop: "Reserved" column.

In the gap between when an item sells and when it ships, it will occupy the "Reserved" column of your "FBA Inventory" page. It may sit there for days depending on the shipping option the buyer chose, but most will become a full-blown sale (read: convert to money in your account) in short time.

There are three reasons items posted there will not convert to a sale:

1. The buyer's card gets declined.
2. The item is being measured by Amazon.

3.   The item is being returned to you because you placed a removal order for it.

What does the second one mean? If you sent in an obscure item that Amazon has never seen in one of its warehouses, it is placed on reserved status while Amazon measures its dimensions and weight. This is important to remember; I was fooled into a false sense of having made a large sale a dozen times only to be let down before I realized what was happening.

The third means that when you ask Amazon to remove an item and return it to you (for whatever reason), it sits in limbo in your reserve for a while before it's shipped out.

Third stop: Your inbox.

When the item is in the hands of UPS, you will receive an e-mail from Amazon stating that they have shipped an order for you.

How much did I make?

The e-mail will not mention the amount you made on the sale. To see that, look for the "Payment Summary" sidebar on the main page of your seller's account, and click on the balance. That will bring you to a page that breaks down each sale in the payment period and displays your cut of the sale.

REPRICING

11

MANUAL REPRICING
ROBOT REPRICING

MAKING REPRICING WORK

There are two ways to reprice: manually, or by using a repricing program.

Repricing is a double-edged sword. You get to optimize your prices to increase sales, but so does everyone else—leading a downward spiral to penny-book territory. This is why responsible repricing always **matches** the lowest price, never undercuts it.

The biggest mistake people make when repricing is trying to have the lowest price. With exceptions (supra-million-ranking books for instance), this is unnecessary and shortsighted.

I'll reiterate that I'm not a proponent of looking at each inventory item as a fragile baby that must be frequently coddled and attended to until it grows up and leaves the nest. I like my inventory feral. I price it once, and very occasionally go back and run checks on old inventory. Your overall emphasis should be on new, quality inventory; not yesterday's news. Most of it will sell eventually—without your overbearing mothering habits.

With those points in mind, here's a brief look at both repricing methods...

Manual repricing

Phase I
Click on the "Inventory" tab, and check the box for "Active." This brings up all your open listings.

Go to "Preferences," in the upper right. You want to check the boxes next to sales rank, price, lowest price, available, product name, and status. There is other useful data that can be displayed, but we'll keep it simple here.

Under "Show shipping charges in Price columns," set to "Display Shipping Charges in Your Inventory's Price Columns."

Set the "Default Filter Option" to "All Fulfillment Channels."

We have told Amazon to compare our FBA offers against prices for all offers, not just FBA.

Why did we do this, when I advise competing against FBA offers only? Remember the caveat: I advise this *except* with poorly-ranked books. And most non-book media categories. That's what we're focused on in Phase 1.

You will see the sales rank in the far right column, and beside it either a green check indicating you have the top spot (lowest price) in the listings, or the price you need to match to capture that spot.

Now you're going to go through your offers, and when you don't see that green check, click "Match Price" for the following offers:

- Anything ranked worse than 1.2 million.
- Any CD ranked worse than 10,000.
- Any other non-DVD media (VHS, cassettes, etc).
- Anything that is *not* a textbook (Textbooks are seasonal, and 1.2 million isn't that bad in the off season).

Hit "Submit." You just made all your lower-demand books and long tail media items competitively priced.

Remember this formula is entirely personal. And while I advise it, your formula may be different.

Phase II

Now we're going to reprice our more well-ranked media.

Go back to the "Preferences" tab in the upper-right. Set the "Default Filter Option" to "Fulfilled by Amazon." Now, only your FBA competition is displayed.

Now you go through your listings again, this time clicking over to Amazon for each offer to view your FBA competition, and reprice (either up or down) according to your personal pricing formula.

Repricing software

With great power comes great responsibility. Remember this as you set an unthinking program in motion that will drop prices, competing against other programs also dropping prices. If it sounds like a recipe for disaster, it can be. Perhaps the biggest factor in the deadly "race to the bottom" is repricers running wild by unknowing or uncaring users.

With that disclaimer, repricing programs are tremendous assets to an FBA business when used **responsibly**.

That last word is key. Repricing programs are the likely culprit when you occasionally see FBA offers for one penny—someone let his repricer go wild, didn't set the proper parameters, and it ran the price straight down to the floor. (P.S. I predict sometime soon in the blogosphere, if not in the mainstream news, you will read a story about a repricer run wild, and the shrewd customer who purchased 3,500 books for $35—with free shipping, of course).

Here are a few repricers currently on the market:

- Teikametrics
- Solid Commerce
- My Repricer
- Seller Engine
- RepriceIt
- FBA Repricer
- Feedvisor

I've played around with most of these and found them to have massive blindspots.

Here is the biggest thing to know about repricing software: Just like your scanning app, they cannot "see" FBA offers that are not priced in the bottom 20.

Many repricing software companies claim their repricer has no such blindspots. They're lying. As of this writing, no repricing software has the ability to circumvent Amazon's rules about accessing FBA offers - despite what they might claim.

Except for repricing your lower demand items (where other FBA offers are not a consideration), repricing software is virtually worthless.

If you did opt to use it, when is it time to use software? My advice: Around the time your inventory hits 1,000 individual listings, manually repricing starts to become difficult.

That said, as of this writing I have abandoned use of all repricing software for its aforementioned irrelevance to FBA sellers.

In previous editions of this book, I endorsed one particular repricer. I am refraining from doing so now for several reasons:

1. That repricer was (and still is) such a mess, with so many unforgivable glitches and such abominable customer service, that it shouldn't be on the market.

2. They lied about their ability to reprice FBA offers, which I found out the hard way.

3. My needs may be different than your needs, and there is no "one size fits all" solution to repricing. Some people need a very nuance-receptive repricer, whereas others demand simplicity and the fewest possible variables (I don't recommend FBA media-sellers sellers take the latter route).

4. Repricers come and go and change often, and any repricer I might recommend today may not be the one I recommend next month.

If you must use software, all offer free trials, so test them out and use them wisely.

ADVANCED TRICKS FOR MANAGING FEEDBACK

12

GETTING TO KNOW YOUR FEEDBACK RATING
HOW TO HAVE BAD FEEDBACK REMOVED
FEEDBACK REMOVAL II: THE LAST RESORT
HOW I RAISED MY FEEDBACK TWO POINTS IN TWO WEEKS

CUSTOMER FEEDBACK AND THE FBA SELLER

Another FBA advantge: Selling with Fulfillment by Amazon greatly limits the reasons people can leave you negative feedback (Amazon takes responsibility for most of the things that can go wrong). If you're having feedback issues, FBA can be the cure.

However, there are feedback pitfalls unique to FBA that are worth looking at.

The primary feedback pitfall for FBA sellers

Complaints about quality are still a very real threat for FBA sellers. Prime Subscribers pay more and expect more. Most of my negative feedback has been for blemishes to the book that were clearly explained in my condition description and was apparently overlooked by the buyer.

There is no recourse here but to work something out with the buyer. Amazon will not remove this kind of feedback.

What's more, there is no way for FBA sellers to go back and review their condition description after a sale, allowing no way to provide concrete evidence to a buyer that they overlooked something that was clearly explained. It can be quite maddening.

On the subject of complaints about condition, it's important for FBA sellers to understand the journey their inventory takes. Your item will take a much more circuitous route to its destination than that of a standard seller. So pack your "new" items well, and be aware that if they're teetering on the edge of "used" condition, they'll probably cross that line before they make it to the customer.

Your book has a long, brutal journey from your hands to the buyer's. Bad things happen to books in transit. Your book will take a ride in a box on a couple trucks, get thrown onto a few conveyor belts, and then shelved by warehouse employees. And when the book is ordered, it takes the same trip all over again. Every step brings the opportunity for bumps and creases.

Generally speaking, Prime subscribers can be a little prima donna. Since joining FBA, I have gotten some of the most obnoxious, unwarranted feedback in the history of injustice.

Here are some samples:

- The customer who ordered a book described as "acceptable condition—has some water damage to first chapter," and complained that there was "water damage to the first chapter."
- The customer who ordered a book described as "Good condition, signed by the author," then complained there was "writing on the first page."
- The customer who ordered a VHS copy of *It's a Wonderful Life*, who then complained when she received a VHS copy of *It's a Wonderful Life* (she wanted a DVD).

FEEDBACK MATTERS

I'm giving the issue of responding to bad feedback a lot of space, because it is a serious issue. Amazon will ban you so ruthlessly that (almost) no trick you can think of to hide your identity will get you a new account.

Even one neutral or negative feedback is no small thing and should be addressed vigorously. This is important for two reasons: Feedback affects your standing with Amazon, and feedback affects sales.

As for the first, Amazon is absolutely ruthless about banning sellers who do not meet their customer satisfaction demands. Fall below their target feedback percentage and you'll get a warning. You are expected to turn around your performance **quickly** or you'll be permanently blacklisted.

And by blacklisted, I don't mean having your bank account blocked, forcing you to open another one and start over. I don't even mean Amazon blocking your IP address, forcing you to do business using Starbucks's wifi. I mean you'll have your MAC address (an individual computer's unique identifier) banned, along with your bank account and any you may try to open in the future. I mean a very thorough blacklisting, leaving you unable to sell on Amazon ever again (see the end of this chapter for a source that may offer a workaround).

What's more, the Wall Street Journal estimates 90% of customers purchase what's in the "Buy Box" We can only speculate as to the algorithm that determines which offer gets the "Buy Box," but contrary to popular belief, it does not automatically go to the lowest price. It goes to the seller Amazon believes is most likely to satisfy the customer (assuming their price is *close* to the lowest), and what determines that is your feedback score. To put it bluntly: If you have a low feedback score, you could lose 90% of your sales. That's it.

Your standing with Amazon is based on these performance metrics:

- Order Defect Rate (negative feedback)
- Cancellation Rate
- Late Shipment Rate
- Policy Violations
- On-Time Delivery
- Contact Response Time

If 100% of your inventory is FBA, the only thing you have to worry about is not getting bad feedback (otherwise defined as "making your customers happy"), not getting caught breaking rules, and responding to customers promptly.

FEEDBACK RATING: THE DANGER ZONE

When will Amazon kick you off? What ultimately defines whether Amazon kicks you off is your Order Defect Rate, defined by Amazon as "*...the number of orders with a defect divided by the number of orders in the time period of interest. It is represented as a percentage.*"

For an FBA seller, an "order defect" is simply code for negative feedback. Watch your feedback. Amazon offers these cautionary words to anyone who lets their feedback fall below 96%:

❝Amazon's Performance Targets state that, 'the number of negative feedback entries should be less than 5% of the total feedback entries received.' If your negative feedback rate is greater than the 5% performance target, you may want to review your business practices and adjust to the demands of customers."

You may not read it this way, but that's Amazon's version of a veiled threat.

The curse of neutral feedback

Ultimately, buyers base their trust in you on the percentage number next to your seller name. That number is the percentage of positive feedback. This means both negative and neutral feedback counts against this figure. The truth is that nearly every buyer will read "97% positive feedback" as "3% negative feedback." They don't see that 3% for what it is: 3% negative *and* neutral. And some happy customers will still leave neutral feedback.

Here is the good news about neutral feedback: It does not count towards your order defect rate—only negative feedback does. That "defect rate" metric is the one that ultimately determines whether or not Amazon allows you to have selling privileges.

So neutral feedback does count with getting the trust of the buyer. It does not count in the eyes of Amazon.

GETTING MILITANT ABOUT FEEDBACK

Here's Amazon's official response to the question: *How do I respond to negative feedback?*:

" Ask the buyer to remove the feedback. If you want to respond to negative feedback, the best option is to work with the buyer to improve the situation that led to the negative feedback. Then, ask the buyer to remove the feedback. To do this, contact the buyer with concern over the problem, and remedy it if possible. If you develop a positive relationship, ask the buyer to remove the feedback. Instructions on how to remove feedback can be found on our buyer Help page, Leaving Feedback. When contacting a buyer, always keep in mind that pressuring a buyer is unacceptable and a violation of our policies."

So you can't "pressure" a buyer. But what **can** you do?

HOW TO HAVE FEEDBACK REMOVED

First, the easy low-hanging fruit. You're not breaking any rules with this one.

As an FBA seller, when feedback is the result of something that is clearly Amazon's fault, they will remove it. Examples include complaints about late shipping or items not arriving.

Amazon will remove feedback if any of these apply:

- If the comment is about a late or lost package (Amazon or UPS's fault)
- If the comment contains obscene language.
- If the comment reveals personally identifying information, like an address.
- If the entire comment is a product review, such as "this book is poorly written" (this actually happens).
- Feedback complaining about an item's price.

You contact Seller Support, point them to the offending feedback, and it it will be examined and removed - sometimes instantly.

Now, how do we deal with the rest? Answer: bribery.

Hacking feedback: Black hat feedback removal tactics

Your approach to feedback removal must conform to the reality of FBA. The two relevant issues here are:

1. Offering anything on the condition that the buyer removes feedback is strictly forbidden.
2. All e-mails are routed through, and potentially read by, Amazon.

So you have to do a little dance that doesn't involve bribing customers into removing feedback. Instead you'll be invoking the rule of reciprocity—a "no strings" gesture in hopes that they will return the favor.

I send the customer an e-mail that reads:

"Hi (first name)

I just learned from the feedback you left that you were unsatisfied with (name the item).

Making people happy is our business, but sometimes we make mistakes. I'd like offer you one of two things to make up for it.

• A free $10 gift card (good for anything on Amazon).
• A full refund AND a $10 gift card (if you'd like to send the item back to us).

Please let me know if either of these options would be acceptable, or what else I can do and I'll take care of it.

146

(Name)"

They'll usually respond, and usually choose the second option. Then I order a $10 gift card, choose the "deliver by e-mail" option, and have it delivered to their "@marketplace.amazon.com" e-mail address.

Then I send the follow-up:

> *"I just sent you the gift card [or: issued the full refund] and you should see it in your inbox [back in your account] right away.*
>
> *If you're happy with the way I've settled this, I would be extremely grateful if you'd consider reversing your feedback.*
>
> *Feedback can be resolved in about 10 seconds at this link:*
>
> *https://www.amazon.com/gp/css/order-history*
>
> *1. Click "Order Details" in the left-hand column, under the "Order Placed" date.*
> *2. Scroll down to Your Seller Feedback and click Remove. The Remove Feedback page appears.*
> *3. Select a reason, and then click Remove Feedback.*
>
> *The gift card [or refund] is yours to keep either way. But I really like happy endings and feedback is really important to small sellers like me, so I'd really appreciate it. If there's any reason you're still not satisfied, please let me know what else I can do and I'll take care of it.*
>
> *Thanks for being an awesome customer!*
>
> *(Your name / your store name)"*

About 65% of the time, the feedback is gone in 24 hours.

If not, I follow up with a polite reminder of how grateful I would be if they would consider removing the feedback, and include instructions again. I follow up with the same e-mail several times at intervals of ten days or so until the feedback is removed (or until they tell me to leave them alone).

Buyers can remove feedback for up to sixty days. If after six weeks the buyer has failed to do so, I send a rather short and groveling e-mail stating bluntly that I've made every attempt to make this right, that negative feedback can be devastating to an online seller, and that their feedback caused my rating to drop by a whole point. And would you **please** consider removing your feedback? Then I paste instructions, again.

There have been a couple of times when I've finally gotten a response after the sixth or seventh e-mail, and had feedback removed with days to spare.

A note on persistence: If at any point the customer responds and says *"Leave me alone,"* concede defeat. Amazon is watching and it's best to avoid any "harassment of customers" while there are witnesses.

THE LAST RESORT: THE REVERSE FEEDBACK SNIPER STATISTIC MANIPULATION TECHNIQUE

You finally got there: Negative feedback has hit 5% and you're on the precipice of disaster. At any moment Amazon could put you on probation, which is so deep down the danger road, it's time for desperate measures.

Here we go.

I found myself in this situation once, receiving four negative feedbacks in quick succession. There is a cascading effect to negative feedback. When people see the last guy left negative feedback, they follow suit like robotic zombie sheep when their feedback may otherwise have been positive.

My entire income was on the line. I had thousands of items in my inventory. Death was knocking at my door. I started doing some math.

I had 750 feedback ratings over the past 365 days. Thirty-seven negative or neutral ratings to 713 positive. That put me at 95% positive. Danger zone.

How I reversed my fate in two weeks

I wanted to get my feedback up to 97% immediately. I could expect thirty new ratings during in the next two weeks.

780 positive : 37 negative = 95%

One of the negative ratings was going to become over 365 days old and would no longer count towards my percentage.

780 positive : 36 negative = 95%

If I received no further negative feedback ratings, I could expect positive ratings to increase at a rate of two per day over the two weeks.

802 positive : 36 negative = 96%

Meanwhile, fifteen positive ratings would become older than 365 days and not count towards my figure.

788 positive : 36 negative = 95%

I sent an extremely groveling e-mail to every person who left negative or neutral feedback in the past sixty days explaining that my entire livelihood was in jeopardy because of their feedback. This yielded exactly one removed rating.

788 positive : 35 negative = 96%

The next step: soliciting positive feedback from customers. I went through every order from the last ninety days to send direct messages to customers requesting positive feedback. The risk here was that in soliciting feedback, I would be waking sleeping giants who would be moved to leave bad feedback they otherwise would have forgotten about. So I wanted to increase my chances by only contacting customers who would have the highest likelihood of having positive things to say. I reasoned there were high risk categories for defective and imperfect products, and decided not to contact customers who bought the following:

- CDs (returns for seemingly perfect CDs that skip are high, and a lot of cases crack in transit)
- DVDs (same reason)
- New books (too much potential for damage in transit)

I e-mailed every customer who bought used books or non-media and requested they leave feedback if they were happy with their purchase. I included instructions how to leave a feedback rating. Total e-mails sent: 2,400. Total positive ratings received: 118 (just under 5%).

906 positive : 35 negative = 96%

I needed 150 more positive ratings to be comfortably in the 97% slot. This is where I got bold.

I drafted an e-mail with a link to my Amazon store and sent it to hundreds of personal contacts, offering one of two things:

1. Any item I was selling for $5 or less for **free** (I had about 400 items in this range.)
2. Five dollars off anything I was selling.

The first 150 people to buy a book and e-mail me the receipt, would get $5. The only stipulation was: They had to leave positive feedback.

I sent this out to my entire address book of personal contacts, and broadcasted it on Facebook, Twitter, and everywhere else.

The majority (a hundred or so) were friends I reached out to personally who had no interest in a free book; they just wanted to help.

By the end of two weeks, after some vigorous follow-up, my feedback hit 97%.

I never ran the exact numbers, but after averaging about $1.50 per book in Amazon reimbursement, I estimate the entire operation cost close to $525— a very small price to pay for preserving a business that was bringing in that amount every 48 hours.

EPILOGUE

To prevent another crisis, I took rigorous stock of mistakes that had led to this and massively overhauled my buying and grading criteria.

I learned several things:

1. Selling heavily damaged books as Acceptable isn't worth it, no matter how clear your description. Many buyers will buy books without reading your description.

2. Selling slightly damaged non-media items isn't worth it, no matter how clear your description. See above.
3. It pays to grade conservatively. List Like New books as Very Good, Very Good books as Good, and so on. It only takes one unreasonable customer to leave bad feedback.
4. Even as a volume seller, you have to check books thoroughly for writing, highlighting, and missing supplemental material (e.g. CDs and inserts.)

Since then, I have raised my score further, and held it at 98% (a good percentage for Amazon sellers) ever since.

IF YOU GET KICKED OFF AMAZON...

...you may have an option. And for that, you have to respect the world's hackers and hacker-minded for creating workarounds for everything.

Remember that when Amazon blacklists you, they **really** blacklist you. Amazon will block not your IP, but your computer itself (via the MAC address), any bank account you have now, and any bank account you set up in an attempt to be sneaky.

I now refer you to an e-book titled *Amazon Ghost*. Though I cannot vouch for it, the book claims to offer step-by-step instruction for blacklisted sellers on setting up a new account under Amazon's radar. I have fortunately never been in a position to need this information. For those less fortunate, the book can be found at the *Amazon Ghost* website (*akpkin.com*).

Endnote: Feedback Mastery - The Book

Feedback is serious, and to address the issue in full I published a greatly expanded version of this chapter as its own ebook. It's titled *Feedback Mastery: The Amazon Annihilation Feedback Repair System*. When I say "greatly expanded," I mean it. It's 50 pages covering every aspect of Amazon feedback, how to maintain it, and how to repair it.

EXIT STRATEGIES: TURNING DEAD INVENTORY INTO PROFIT

13

DEALING WITH THE LEFTOVER AND THE UNWANTED

SOLUTIONS FOR DUSTY OR UNSELLABLE INVENTORY

After your first year, despite diligent repricing, a certain percentage of your inventory just won't sell.

You took a chance on *Applied Cryptography*. You shipped three copies to Amazon, only one sold, and now you're looking for a way out.

The first, and only widely discussed option is to create a disposal order. On your FBA account interface, you tell Amazon which items you no longer want to have in your inventory, and for 15¢ per unit, they hurl them into a flaming volcano.

This prevents you from continuing to pay storage fees on the item. However, it does nothing to recoup past storage fees, the cost of the item, or other small costs incurred during the item's lifespan.

There is another option.

Plan A: Hold a fire sale

When a book doesn't sell, it is not always due to lack of demand. Often the book is just priced higher than the market can bear. There is one way to test for this: Cut the price in half.

Every time I have a book in inventory for over two years and it's priced more than $10, I will cut the price in half. And something interesting often happens. That book that "no one wants" sells—quickly.

I will regularly halve the price of a poorly-selling book, only to see it sell within a few weeks, and sometimes the same day.

Who is buying these books? It may be an enterprising book dealer who thinks I have undervalued the book and thinks they can resell at a profit. Maybe they can. We simply have different expectations: I would prefer $50 today to $100 in 2027, and he would prefer the $100 when the temperature in Hell reaches thirty-two degrees. Or he may already have a buyer lined up. Either way, we're both happy. I'll take the money and be on to the next thing.

The buyer may also be someone who has a certain price threshold and checks in on the book frequently (or has an e-mail alert set up with a book price comparison site like *booksprice.com*), waiting for it to drop to a price within his comfort zone. And when it does, he swoops in.

Or there may be hundreds of people clamoring for the book, and none of them are willing to pay anything close to the current used Amazon price. But cut the price in half, and a few of them will be interested. Then you get the sale.

I've done it countless times to old book languishing in inventory. Cut the price in half, and the book sells.

When a book is ranked 8 million, it doesn't mean someone is showing an interest in the book only once a year. It means someone is only **buying** it once a year. What prevents the people who look but don't buy from purchasing is often a price they consider exorbitant.

I don't like the precedent set by dramatically underpricing your competition (throwing into motion the deadly race to the bottom, where sellers underprice each other into the bargain basement). That said, if a book hasn't sold in a year or two, there is something wrong, and it's the right time to pull whatever power move you must to turn the book into money.

Plan B: Purge the books too cheap to discount.

Then there are the books whose sales ranks and prices drop through the floor, creating inventory clutter that is, by every useful measure, a liability. Dropping prices significantly means you're selling books at a gross-profit loss; and they're also racking up storage fees. You need a way out.

Amazon offers you two options: dispose or remove.

Creating a disposal order: This is where you tell Amazon to take your item and throw it away. I don't really know what they do with these items, but I've spent a lot of time fantasizing about checking out the dumpsters behind one of the FBA warehouses just because I think it would be interesting (and profitable).

Here's how you create a disposal order:

1. In your Inventory Amazon Fulfills view, check the box(es) next to the items you want to be rid of.
2. Through the drop down menu, select Create a Disposal Order.
3. Click through a few more pages, and you don't ever have to see (or pay

for) the item again.

The cost is 15¢ per regular item and 30¢ for oversized items.

Creating a removal order: This means you're requesting that Amazon ship items from your inventory back to you. If you think you can sell the item elsewhere or you want it for yourself, this method will bring it to your door in about a week. They do this for the unbelievably low price of 50¢ per regular item, 60¢ for oversize. It's an incredibly generous rate.

Follow the same steps as above, but instead select Create a Removal Order.

DEALING WITH LEFTOVERS

If you're finding bulk sources (and you should), you will invariably find yourself burdened with a lot of "dead wood." These are the books of no value that must be dealt with eventually.

I have no doubt there is a certain karmic tax to throwing a good book in a dumpster, and I prefer to find most of my leftovers good homes. I collect leftovers in a walk-in closet until I have a thousand or more, then do one of the following:

1. Put an ad on Craigslist. I'll offer 1,000+ books for $50 with a photo and see if anyone bites.
2. Put a simultaneous auction on eBay. I'll list the auction for pickup only and cancel if I get a Craigslist buyer.
3. Pay a neighborhood kid to oversee a garage sale. I'll advertise "Thousands of books!" on Craigslist and *YardSaleSearch.com*, charge 50¢ per book or three for a dollar, collect my profits at the end, and recycle the rest.
4. Group everything by subject and sell them as eBay lots (shipped Media Mail). It is difficult to sell a shippable quantity of mixed-subject books, but lots comprised of specific subjects or authors do well.

I recently sold a lot of fifty books on the Egyptian pyramids for $91. Individually, every title was a penny book and ranked worse than 2 million. As a lot, they were a great deal for someone with a passion for this topic.

As a last resort, I'll post under the Free section of Craigslist. Do this and you will get one hundred emails in six hours. This is the most time-efficient route, yet least profitable.

POST–MEDIA:
TAKING FBA ALL THE WAY

14

SELLING ANYTHING WITH FBA
POST-MEDIA MODELS
BUYING AMAZON REAL ESTATE

INCREASING YOUR RANGE: CAN YOU SELL ANYTHING VIA FBA?

Yes.

We started you with books and media because they are abundant and inexpensive. In time, you may want to graduate from media to literally anything else with a bar code.

The full scope of possibility with FBA is outside the range of this book, but it's worth giving a taste of the options available to anyone who wants to break through the media ceiling towards a landscape of limitless profit.

Read this list and consider whether you know of a cheap wholesale or discount retail source for anything in any of these categories. You can turn over items from these categories for big profits via FBA:

- Baby Products
- Beauty
- Camera & Photo
- Cell Phones & Accessories
- Consumer Electronics
- Grocery & Gourmet Food
- Health & Personal Care
- Home & Garden
- Pet Supplies
- Kitchen
- Musical Instruments
- Office Products
- Personal Computer
- Software
- Sports & Outdoors
- Tools & Home Improvement
- Toys & Games
- Video Games
- Video Game Consoles

For merchant-fulfilled sellers,, most of these categories require approval to get "featured merchant" status (the only way to be profitable). Fortunately for us, approval for many of these is automatic for FBA sellers.

The following categories require approval to sell in, even as an FBA seller:

- Automotive

158

- Clothing
- Collectible books
- DVDs
- Entertainment collectibles
- Fine Art
- Industrial and Scientific
- Luggage
- Appliances
- Sexual Wellness
- Shoes
- Sports Collectibles
- Watches
- Wine

POST-MEDIA MODELS

Choose to move beyond media and you enter an almost limitless expanse of opportunity.

If you can get your hands on it, you can list it. And someone will probably buy it. Maybe a lot of it.

Here are a few models (of many) to consider, all of which are making people money on Amazon right now:

Retail Arbitrage
As popularized by the book *Retail Arbitrage*, this is the practice of using scanning apps to source products from retail stores and selling them on Amazon at a profit. Seriously, you can do this. And what's better about this compared to most used media sources is that when you find a profitable item, you can take home five or ten or a hundred of them. Popular sources include Big Lots, TJ Max, and anywhere selling clearance or discounted items.

Private Labeling
There are some high-end courses that cover this subject in detail. The recipe goes like this: Find a manufacturer, slap your own label on it, sell it on Amazon. Done.

Sourcing from China
Exactly like it sounds: Finding items not on Amazon and sourcing them directly from the source of almost everything: China.

Buying Wholesale

This is identifying products you would like to sell, tracking down a wholesale source (a manufacturer or a middleman), and buying in bulk.

BUYING UP AMAZON REAL ESTATE

If you don't see a listing for something on Amazon and you think others are searching for it, you have found a big opportunity. There are two versions of this scenario: items not on Amazon that already have a UPC, and items not on Amazon that do **not** have a UPC.

If you find an item that already has a UPC and is not on Amazon, **and** you believe others are searching for it, jump on the opportunity to create a product page. Go to Add a Product and then Create a New Product. You can enter the item's UPC,

Non-media blind spot food

The biggest non-media blind spot I've found is food. There are two large overstock stores in my area that rarely price items that allow room for profit on Amazon (one even sells on Amazon). Both have only one profitable section: overstock grocery.

Even sellers who think outside of the media box don't often think to sell food. The sources for discounted food are plentiful. Consider grocery outlet stores, of which every city has at least one. And have you seen the show *Extreme Couponing*, in which savvy coupon clippers walk out with ten carts of groceries for $1.50? Tremendous arbitrage opportunity.

Harmony Valley Vegetarian Sausage Mix, 5.7-Ounce (Pack of 6)
by Harmony Valley

Price: $23.54 ($0.69 / oz) Prime

Only 12 left in stock (more on the way).
Ships from and sold by Amazon.com. Gift-wrap available.

Want it delivered Saturday, January 5? Order it in the next 15 hours and 19 minutes, and choose Saturday Delivery at checkout. Details

Pay only $22.36 ($0.65 / oz) and relax with Subscribe & Save.
Sign up for automatic deliveries of this item and get an extra 5% discount.
No fees, no obligations, and shipping is always FREE. Details
Subscribe & Save now available with the latest Amazon Mobile App for iPhone & Android.

4 new from $23.54

New Year, New You
Get a healthy start to 2013 with deals on healthy and organic products from top vendors such as Kashi, Nutiva, Splenda, Kind Snacks, South Beach Diet, Quaker, thinkThin, Campbell's Soup Company, Lipton and Fiji Water. Shop all.

Product Features
- Pack of six, 5.7-ounce packages (total of 34.2 ounces)
- Soy based, vegan and kosher certified meat alternative that makes eating less meat, or eating meat-less easy and versatile
- Just add cold water, refrigerate for 15 minutes, and cook
- Great source of protein and fiber
- Same consistency and versatility as ground meat

add your own image and description, and the page will be live instantly.

You can also brainstorm items that are not on Amazon and which do not already have UPCs. This can be a single item or an original bundle of complimentary items that you assemble yourself. Barcodes can be purchased many places, but the cheapest I place I know of are the bulk barcode sellers on eBay.

For a much more detailed explanation of this subject, again check out the book *Arbitrage*.

THE FORMULA

I have a circuit of discount, salvage, and overstock stores I shop in my area. These stores make me a respectable side-income independent of my media sales. It is a very different business than selling media, with its own benefits and drawbacks. On my journey into non-media, I have found the margins are generally smaller. Yet when you find an item that will bring you a 300% or greater profit (as per my personal rule), you can buy multiples.

There are two questions before you as you get started in post-media FBA models:

1. What are local places where I can source products cheaply?
2. What can I buy wholesale or otherwise source that is not on Amazon right now?

People are making big money being the sole seller of niche products or bundles on Amazon. You will have your best ideas in niches you know well. Think about your passions and what products people who share your passions are seeking. Find items on that list that are not on Amazon, and try to get in at ground floor by creating your own product page.

The opportunities here are huge (and again, outside the scope of this book). This is the short recipe:

1. Find items that are not on Amazon **or** bundle like items together in unique ways.
2. Buy a barcode if needed.
3. Create a product page.
4. Repeat.

That's the formula.

INCREASING THE VALUE OF YOUR ITEMS: A FEW BLACK HAT TRICKS

15

MANIPULATING THE VALUE OF YOUR ITEMS
DAMAGE CONTROL

TRICKS FOR INCREASING THE VALUE OF YOUR BOOKS & MEDIA

Disclaimer: I am not advising anything for which I have ever received negative feedback.
Disclaimer II: One or two of these tricks are against the rules.

Here are a couple "Amazon hacks" that will give value to otherwise worthless items. (If Amazon ever reads this and figures out who I am, this chapter alone will get me banned from selling.)

Listing older editions as new

Disclaimer III: You can really upset a customer (and do damage to her grade in school) by misusing this tactic. Never do this with textbooks.

This works with two kinds of books: classics that haven't changed in decades (or centuries), and books sneakily repackaged by publishers as a new edition with <u>absolutely no substantive changes</u> or updates made (e.g. *The Expectant Father* series).

When I'm not depriving a buyer of any value by doing so, I will not hesitate to list older editions as newer editions. I do this most often with classics. For example, I will readily list a Penguin Classics edition of *The Iliad* from 1990 with the Penguin Classics edition from 1998. The content hasn't

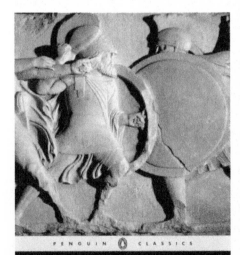

changed for thousands of years. An eight-year discrepancy on the printing date isn't hurting anyone.

Damage control: Rolling back the clock on blemished books

I buy new-condition books that aren't "new" and list them as new, and you will too. I also repair damaged books that aren't new and list them as new, and you will too.

It's not a crime because 1) it's victimless, and 2) it's not a crime. If a book is cosmetically flawless, the number of previous owners is purely academic.

Here are the most common blemishes you will find along with workarounds for each:

Ink in the corner of a title page (e.g. price marked in pen, owner's name, etc): I snip the corner off with scissors and in the description note: "Price clip on title page." Experienced sellers are screaming at this page right now, but the stats don't lie; I've never gotten negative feedback for this. A price clip is a disfigurement found on older remainder and overstock books in which the corner of the dust jacket flap has a corner snipped off. I just extend the definition by one page. No harm, no foul. *Note: Don't do this with collectible books.*

Price written inside in pencil: Some library bookstores and thrift stores will pencil a price on the first page. If an eraser still leaves a ghost image behind, I'll write a 1, 2, or 3 in front of the price to get close to or over the cover price, then erase that. If the buyer was to notice the faint pencil residue of the original price, he would see a price that would make him feel like he's been duped by paying $20 for a 50¢ book. By adding a digit, if he sees "$20" penciled in a book he just paid $7 for, he feels like he got one over on *you*.

Writing inside book: I'm stating the obvious here, but pencil marks can be removed with an eraser. The vast majority of books written in are only marked on the first few pages. (Did you know less than 10% of books ever get read past the first chapter? Incredible.)

Ink marks and other blemishes on cover: WD-40 is pure magic. It removes (almost) everything. I use it every day. It's like kryptonite to ink. You won't believe it.

Dustjackets and covers that have lost their shine or have faint scratches, giving them a used look: Do a once-over with rubbing alcohol and a rag, then give a light application of Vaseline; a dab of it on a soft clean cloth can restore shine to dust jackets. Wipe it on and wipe it off.

Writing and other blemishes on a single functionless page (like blank page, redundant title page, etc.): This is common. Someone writes his name on the title page rendering an otherwise new book not new. If it is not taking value from the book, I will use a razor to cut out the page right at the spine. If done correctly, it can be almost undetectable. But do this flawlessly or not at all—if detected, this begs for bad feedback.

Stains and blemishes on the back cover: FBA saves the day here. FBA labels can be used to cover all sorts of offensive imperfections.

Remainder marks: These are generally a black pen mark swiped across the edge of the book, commonly found on books designated as overstock or remainder titles. These are dealt with by ignoring them and denoting "Has remainder mark" front and center in your description. Light sandpaper will also remove remainder marks.

"Used" stickers on textbooks: This is a very common problem remedied by Goo Gone. Get some. This is a miracle of WD-40 proportions. Also recommended: the Scotty Peeler Label & Sticker Remover: These are perfect for removing labels from books. Available on Amazon and worth the investment.

(For advanced book restoration techniques, see my upcoming book: *Condition Hacking*, probably out by the time you read this.)

Damage control II: Rolling back CDs & DVDs

Scratched DVDs and CDs can be one of the quickest ways to get bad feedback. What looks like a small blemish that is no cause for concern can make for an unplayable disc.

You have two options:

1. Take the discs somewhere that offers a disc repair service. Used CD and video game stores often offer disc repair and charge about a dollar per disc.

2. Purchase a disc repair machine. If you're going to deal in volume, go this route. The JFJ Easy Pro Universal CD/DVD Repair Machine is a respected machine that can be purchased new on Amazon for $120. I have one, and its awesome.

Consider the value of your time, and don't drive across town to repair a five dollar DVD. If you have something of value and are unsure if you should invest in having it repaired, try a free downloadable utility called Nero Discspeed. It will scan a CD for errors and takes about one minute per disc.

THE NEXT LEVEL: ADVANCED FBA TACTICS

16

MULTI-CHANNEL FULFILLMENT
ADVANCED FBA METRICS
WINNING THE BUY BOX
TAKING FBA ON THE ROAD

LEVERAGING AMAZON'S WAREHOUSE SPACE TO SELL EVERYTHING, EVERYWHERE: "MULTI-CHANNEL FULFILLMENT"

"Multi-channel fulfillment" is e-commerce-speak for using Amazon's warehouses to sell products on other websites. Yes, you can do this. When you ship an item to FBA, you can sell it anywhere on the internet: eBay, Half. com, AbeBooks, Buy.com—anywhere.

Here's the major FBA advantage: You can offer Amazon's too-good-to-be-true shipping rates to your customers across every channel. Now, sellers not using FBA (which will be 99% of them) can't compete with your shipping rates, which gives you the advantage—and the sale.

This is a crucial way to differentiate yourself from other sellers, a difficult task in the crowded world of e-commerce. Amazon's low shipping rates are a powerful way to offer something that no other seller can.

The first thing to do is ship everything you're selling on eBay or any other channel to Amazon. Do this just as you would any other item that is intended for sale on Amazon: list it, print labels, create a shipment, and send to an FBA warehouse.

You can even price your items uncompetitively on Amazon (e.g. $500 for every book, as a lot of sellers do) if you have no intention of actually making any sales there. Run the numbers, determine the margins you want, and set your price accordingly. The platform where you will eventually make your sale is irrelevant because Amazon is going to take care of the shipping whether it sells through them or not.

Once your product is safely at the FBA warehouse, you can sell it anywhere and Amazon will ship it for you. It can be through eBay, Buy.com, or even a cash sale from your mom.

Here's how to make that happen:

When the item sells, go to the inventory page of your Amazon seller account. Check the box next to the item and select Create a Fulfillment Order. Enter the ship-to address, follow the outlined steps, and Amazon takes care of the rest.

You'll be charged standard FBA fees: 15% commission + $1 "Pick and Pack" fee + 37¢ per pound for shipping.

Here is another great benefit: The charge to ship the item will generally be about one-half what you would pay UPS for the same package. You're utilizing Amazon's partnership with UPS to get FBA-exclusive rates. This gives you a huge advantage over your competitors, allowing you to makes offers like:

- Free shipping. Work the shipping cost into the cost of the item while killing your competition with the "free shipping" offer.

- Hugely discounted second-day shipping. Charge the same price your competitor charges for Ground, but again use Amazon's UPS rates which no non-FBA seller can compete with.

- Offering the same shipping rates as your competitors. Don't compete on cheaper shipping, but work the discounted UPS costs into your sales price while keeping the same margins.

You will get a tracking number one day later, which you can forward to your customer.

There you go. As an FBA seller, you have destroyed your competition yet again.

COOL PARTS OF THE FBA INTERFACE YOU MIGHT NOT KNOW ABOUT

Selling Coach under the Reports tab

It's useful for many things:

1. Seeing which listings are missing images or descriptions that will increase your chances of a sale. I don't like to micromanage or concern myself with any one book. However, it's worth taking a look to see if you have any expensive items that don't have adequate listing pages. Adding photos and descriptions greatly increases your chance of a sale. I find it worth it to take and upload a picture if I know it will help sell a very expensive item.
2. Upload your seller logo. There are categories in which buying requires more trust than in books, and customers expect to see a company logo. A simple logo helps establish you as a legitimate business.

Business Report under the Reports tab

This gives you so many ways to slice your sales metrics, you can get lost in all the options.

One I didn't know about for a while is the Detail Page and Sales Traffic by Item feature, allowing you to see how many times certain items are viewed by people browsing Amazon. This is extremely useful for one thing: If you see an item that you've had in your inventory for a long time is getting moderate or heavy traffic, this is a clear sign the item is overpriced. People are coming to the page and leaving without making a purchase because the market cannot bear the current price. Use this tool to diagnose overpriced items that are languishing in your inventory.

With every report, there is a very easy-to-miss tab that runs vertically along the right side of the screen, which is marked Columns. Click this for a long list of metrics Amazon will display for you, from refund rates to average selling price.

Fulfillment under the Reports tab

Excel junkies can download many things here, such as various order reports. I won't go down that rabbit hole. Here are some of the more interesting things to see:

Inventory Health
A very cool feature that shows you which items have been in your inventory for a long time, which items are expected to incur long term storage fees, and how much those fees will be.

Recommended Removal
Exactly that: which items Amazon advises are not worth storing in an FBA warehouse. This includes items that have been in the warehouse for a long time, and slow-selling items you have multiples of, which will incur long term storage fees. You should run this report every few months and do a purge of dead-weight inventory.

Cross-Border Inventory Movement
A fun report that shows which of your orders came from overseas (if you're signed up for Amazon Export—and you should be).

Returns

This is a page where you can see a full list of your returns going back 180 days and the reasons buyers gave for returning the items. If you're getting a lot of returns for mistakes being made on your end, this is important information.

THE BUY BOX

The Buy Box is a coveted placement for any listing that increases sales dramatically—if you can get the spot.

ChannelDollars.com describes the Buy Box this way:

❝The Amazon Buy Box is the way Amazon compares like products. Instead of a product listing page with rows of matching results as you would see on a typical CSE, Amazon creates a master product page which incorporates all information known to Amazon, as passed on by eligible sellers of that product. Next, Amazon displays the competitive offers from merchants in the upper right hand portion of the page. The Buy Box contains a single offer and frames the now classic Amazon 'Add to Shopping Cart' button which has been duplicated by webmasters around the world. Below this section, Amazon delivers up the consumer a quick review of competing merchant offers.

❝Owning the buy box' means getting that coveted placement in the top right, which puts your product in the customer's shopping cart when they hit the large 'Add To Cart' button. Everything on the product page is guiding the customer towards this button, and your product."

Here's what you have to know about books and the Buy Box:

• It is estimated that 90% of all sales are made through the Buy Box. If your offer isn't in the Buy Box, it may as well not even be for sale.

• FBA offers get preference for the Buy Box. Yet another huge advantage for FBA sellers.

• With books in "New" condition, only Amazon's offer can have the Buy Box. It doesn't matter how low you price your offer, Amazon won't give it up. For this reason, when the Used and New prices are close, I will often list new books as "Like New," just to get the Buy Box.

How to win the Buy Box (It's not just about the lowest price)

Like all of Amazon's algorithms, there is some mystery as to the exact formula for "winning the buy box," so let's talk about what we know:

First, Amazon wants to direct the customer to the most "desirable" listing. Amazon also knows that price is not always the most important factor in their customers buying decisions. Amazon looks at several factors and aims to give the Buy Box to the most worthy seller.

The second, third, and fourth most "worthy" sellers get the screen real estate below the Buy Box, where Amazon positions other offers with much smaller Add to Cart buttons. These sellers receive significantly less sales than the "owner" of the Buy Box.

Here are the known factors which increase your chances of Buy Box placement:

- Price.
- The offer is fulfilled by Amazon (a requirement for the Buy Box in every category I've sold in).
- Inventory (Having multiples of the item in stock favors heavily.)
- Featured merchant status (Given to all FBA sellers automatically.)
- Refund (Those with lower returns due to merchant error earn favor for the top Buy Box spot.)
- Your feedback score.

When all of these factors are combined, this results in a total value which is then measured against other sellers of the item. The most desirable offer then wins the Buy Box.

As of this writing, I have the Buy Box for a high-selling item. I am beating out sellers with better feedback scores and am selling the item at a slightly higher price. The determining factor seems to be that I have twenty of the item in stock, whereas the other sellers only have one. Naturally, Amazon wants to steer customers to sellers who can fill their demands, and don't want to risk losing a sale should a customer want to order multiples.

There is a column you can add to your seller reports that shows the percentage of the time your offer occupied the Buy Box. Go to Reports, choose Business

Reports, then click the vertical Columns tab. Then check Buy Box Percentage to see how you're faring.

Note: There are some categories in which Amazon will never give up the Buy Box. Rules governing this seem subject to change often, so rather than present a list that's likely to change, I'll just recommend you do your research with all non-media inventory.

Get the Buy Box and you will see your sales spike dramatically. One estimate puts it that the Buy Box gets the sale 75% of the time in non-media categories, 50% in media. AKA it's hot real estate. It's worth re-reading this section to understand how to get there.

THE PORTABLE EMPIRE: FBA AND A LIFE OF PRODUCTIVE NOMADISM

I've had more than a few entrepreneurial pursuits, but since 2003 my rule has always been the same: I have to be able to (mostly) run it from a laptop. If I wanted to be anchored to a fixed physical location, I would just get a desk job and call it a life. But I want more.

Since starting FBA, I've made money from Helena, Montana; Los Angeles; New Orleans; Oberlin, Ohio; Milwaukee; Salt Lake City; Seattle; Boulder, Colorado; and a dozen other towns you've never heard of. When an old friend invited me to New Orleans for Saint Patrick's day, I was there. When I was invited to Oberlin to record a hip hop track, I was there. On a whim, I will wake up and decide to take the Amtrak to Fargo or fly to Tucson – and I do it. And I do it with the security of knowing that while I'm exploring the university library in Bowling Green, or walking the base of Devil's Tower, Amazon is making me money.

I don't travel and make up for lost time when I get home. I travel and make the trips pay for themselves.

Here is how I do it:

Step One: Build the List
(Time required: one hour)

Before every trip, I print these lists for each town:

- Thrift stores from *TheThriftShopper.com* and Google maps.
- Overstock and remainder stores from Google.
- Rummage sales from Craigslist and Google.
- Book sales from *BookSalesFinder.com*.
- Additional book sales for the surrounding three county area via library websites.
- Any good leads on book lots for sale on that city's Craigslist from the past month.
- University surplus auctions via *UniversitySurplus.com* and Google.
- Book lots "for pickup only" on eBay.
- Libraries with bookstores.
- Garage sales from Craigslist (filtered by keyword "book").

Step Two: Distill Down the List
(Time required: 30 minutes)

I'm only going to spend 15% of my time, at most, gathering inventory. I strip down the list to only those spots that appear the most lucrative. I use the best available information to make a judgment. This includes opting for sales that are not on *BookSaleFinder.com* over ones that are (if I'm fortunate enough to have multiple options); emailing Craigslist posters who state "lots of books" for specifics, and using Google Street View to identify the biggest stores.

Step Three: Create a Target Profit Point
(Time required: 15 minutes)

I do the rough math (this isn't a Gulag—don't sweat the details) on travel costs and decide if I'm looking to recoup all expenses, or just mitigate. I'll arrive at a target number and map out a plan to reach it in the fewest possible stops, counting on an average profit of $100 per source.

Step Four: Travel
(Time required: Just relax)

I work shopping into my travel casually and without pressure. Adventure is my focus, profit-pursuit is secondary.

Being in inventory-hunt mode while traveling has allowed me to discover new locations and items I never would have had access to otherwise. (A large University of Washington Press back catalog book sale inside the university library? I'm in.) Through casual shopping while traveling, I have built up a list of lucrative sources in various places I like to visit around the country. Now I enjoy visiting a number of cities where I know I will make back all my travel costs in one to four stops. This "work" is done on my schedule, utilizing my portable toolbox and hotel resources.

This model has brought me a level of freedom that leaves all my friends jealous and asking: *How does he do that?*

Last note: For all the details of my complete system for free travel using Fulfillment by Amazon, see the 32-page mini-sequel to this book—*Amazon Autopilot II: On the Road.*

CONCLUSION

17

A CALL FOR SUSTAINABILITY

RESPECT THE GAME

The FBA money machine will only continue if you respect it. During my relatively short time with FBA, I have seen some megabooksellers jump on board and do serious damage. I've watched careless sellers devalue a good portion of Amazon's inventory through thoughtless pricing practices, forcing the rest of us to follow their degenerative path or miss the sale.

Are megasellers going to ruin FBA, glutting the market with penny books, selling mass quantities often at a loss, and forcing the rest of us into unprofitability? Will they continue their obscene pricing (non-)strategies, diminishing their potential profits by half or more from their ignorance, and pushing our profits down with them?

It's possible they will win. It is also possible they will, a year into their FBA experiment, notice their profits falling through the floor, have no idea why, and abandon the FBA ship for a return to in-house fulfillment.

But it is also possible the megasellers will learn that FBA sellers offer a premium service and can command premium prices. It is possible they can be persuaded by the potential for literally doubling their profits; and thus keep this ship from sinking to a place where those of us left are reduced to bottom-feeders, feeling around for scraps we can sell for pennies.

To bring some small hope to the last scenario, I will be mailing a copy of this book to the top ten worst FBA offenders, those who set their prices as though their next heroin fix depended on it.

Fingers crossed.

PARTING WORDS

Keeping FBA sustainable into the years ahead asks only one thing of you: diversify. Let books and media be your launch point into new niches, with FBA as your foundation.

Having broken free from the rusty cage of post office servitude and anchoring to a fixed physical location, what's important now is:

What are you going to do with this freedom?

180

Anyway, I'm going to the UPS Store...

RESOURCES

I spent the first few years as an Amazon seller flailing around, clueless. Today I work hard to bring Amazon sellers the books and articles I wish I'd had years ago.

Let's be honest: There's a lot of medicore material out there. Between my blog and my books, I always promise zero filler, and 100% dense, actionable information.

FBA Mastery (dot com): My site about all things related to selling books and media on Fulfillment by Amazon. If you don't sell via FBA, there's still tons of useful material here. Sign up for my email list and get regular advice, stories, blunders, triumphs, and adventures as I scour the country for anything I can turn into money on Amazon.

Book Sourcing Secrets Every source of cheap books to sell for huge profits on Amazon. 43 sources for Amazon sellers. This is a road-map for six-figure book sales.

Feedback Mastery: The Amazon Annihilation Feedback Repair System A complete guide to maintaining and repairing your feeedback score on Amazon. 50 pages.

Blindspot Profits: Cashing in on Overlooked Items Every Seller Misses The top 20 types of weird, used things you can re-sell for big profits - that your competition is almost certainly missing.

Coming soon:
- *"Book Sourcing - 1k In A Day"* 3 DVD set
- *Condition Hacking* ebook
- Pricing strategy video + ebook set

WEBSITES
Book to the Future
http://www.booktothefuture.com/
Honest Online Selling
http://jordanmalik.com/blog/
Skip McGraths's Online Seller's Resource
http://www.skipmcgrath.com/newsletters/current.shtml

FBA MASTERY

I launched the FBA Mastery website to serve as a complete resource for selling books and media via FBA. Find tips on advanced FBA bookselling tactics, developments in the world of FBA, sourcing advice, stories, and more.

`www.fbamastery.com`

CPSIA information can be obtained at www.ICGtesting.com
Printed in the USA
BVOW08s2119190516

448561BV00003B/186/P